Contemplative Thoughts in Human Nature

Analytical Observations of Human Destructive Tendencies

T0067128

Contemplative Thoughts in Human Nature

Analytical Observations of Human Destructive Tendencies

Dr. Talib Kafaji

authorHOUSE®

AuthorHouse™ LLC
1663 Liberty Drive
Bloomington, IN 47403
www.authorhouse.com
Phone: 1-800-839-8640

Published by AuthorHouse   09/08/2014

ISBN: 978-1-4969-3472-7 (sc)
ISBN: 978-1-4969-3471-0 (e)

Library of Congress Control Number: 2014914761

Contents

Introduction

The idea for this book came to me through working with the great number of people who have seen me for psychological treatments for the last thirty years. Often, I see people who have strong unconscious hidden desires to destroy themselves, and that has led me to believe that people in general have strong tendencies to be destructive to themselves and to the world around them. For example, look at how much money the world is spending on armament; it is beyond comprehension. Our ideal dream is to leave the world in better condition than when we came to it. Unfortunately, that is not happening right now. It is a romantic thought that we be loving and caring about each other. Sadly enough the prevailing world condition we have created is sheer destruction to ourselves and the world we live in, perhaps beyond repair. We are polluting the environment and filling the planet with all manner of poisons and toxicity, as well as immeasurable greed and selfishness that is hard to tackle.

This book addresses some of the destructive behaviors that afflict the human condition. **One challenging question we may ask is, what is the relationship between the cosmetic industry and the military industry?** We will see through their close relationship that both create toxic waste and damage our environment, as well as drain our natural resources. This book also looks at the industry of health and illness, and the profound influence pharmaceutical companies have on health and illness. Some may say human greed is part of human nature. God installed in us the seed of greed, and it is also God who sent prophets to cultivate our corrupt nature.

If accused of drawing an ugly picture about human nature, I would say yes. God has mentioned in all His holy books that human nature from the start is corrupt. Undoubtedly, mankind also has produced a marvelous culture of art and music, as well as glimpses of kindness and compassion. But overall the dark side of human nature has prevailed since the murder of Abel by his brother, Cain. Since then we have struggled within ourselves to suppress the dark side, but it keeps rearing its head constantly; all of the religious teaching given to us did not make a dent in the human consciousness.

We will also address the slave mentality and how people in general behave like sheep, and want to have a shepherd, such as a dictator to rule them. On rare occasions, we as individuals take our responsibilities seriously. We like to state our own responsibility to others. Because, as Zen puts it, "we are lost in the crowd of our guests". There are so many guests in our lives. The first guests are our own experiences in life, our attachment to our parents, the sense of belonging to a group or society or community, plus our beliefs, our education, as well as our immature ego. This puts enormous demands on us to be other than the way we are. All these guests in our lives can contribute to the neuroses and the psychoses of our daily lives. Thus, we are clearly seeking our destruction, if not consciously, then unconsciously. Therefore, this book focuses on the troubled part of human nature that has removed us from the main purpose of life: to live happily and share our happiness with our fellow humans, by being caring and compassionate toward each other.

Dr.Talib Kafaji
Marrakech, Morocco
August 20, 2014

Chapter One

The beginning of human dysfunction:

The Psychology of Adam and Eve

When Almighty God created Adam and put in him the divine spirit of life, perhaps God's intention was to look at His marvelous creation and see His ultimate beauty and miracle in one creature. Then, God instilled in newly-created man the malicious and wicked intentions, which are manifested as greed, envy, jealousy, hate, anger, aggression, and poor self-control. God also instilled in man the benevolent and good intentions which are manifested as love, kindness, creativity, compassion, and giving, as well as the motivation to make the world a better place for his fellow man. Adam stayed by himself and looked around and found that he was lonely. He went to God complaining, "Please, God, I cannot stay by myself. I am terribly lonely. And I need a way to deal with boredom."

God found Adam's request reasonable and created Eve. She was the last of God's creations in this incredible universe. Thus, God put in her the marvels of His creation; she is truly an amazing creature anatomically, far superior in the way she sees life than man. She is very pragmatic, very realistic, has strong self-control, and is comprehensive in the way she perceives the world around her. Moreover, she is less emotional than man; this is why she lives longer than man and has fewer heart attacks or diseases.

Then Almighty God rewarded Adam with Eve. Upon her arrival, poor Adam's life changed drastically, because he was not aware of what he asked for. She animated his life and gave a different taste to the things around him. Adam was very delighted to see Eve around him, and she asked him to make love to her. He was not familiar with such pleasure, so she showed him how to do it. He proclaimed, "This is so delicious and very tantalizing!" And Eve said, "We will have more of it and any time that you want me, I will be there for you. We are a happy couple, newly discovering our new home in Heaven. Then, Adam more or less "freaked out", because they had discovered the physical dimension. Adam at that point literally lost the faculty of reasoning, and became slave to his pleasure with Eve.

Adam and Eve are discovering a new dimension for their life together, that being the mystery of the flesh, by making love to one another. Before this they were just mere soul; now there is a carnal domination that adds to their existence.

Undoubtedly, this began our suffering, because our bodies demand pleasure, and pleasure or the desire for it is the cause of all of our pain, according to Buddha. We can see that clearly manifested in the journey of mankind. Indeed, pleasure can give us glimpses of happiness, but happiness tends to be transient and we keep searching for it most of our lives.

Adam and Eve took a walk around Heaven and smelled the flowers and sampled all the varieties of fruits and vegetables. Of course, there were no animals, so basically our parents, Adam and Eve, were vegetarian. They lived very healthy lives.

Then jealousy started to develop from other creatures around them in Heaven, and the creatures wondered why God gave this couple such privileges. "What do they have that we do not have?" they asked. Clearly, they had observed God's preferential treatment of the couple.

God sensed what had transpired among the inhabitants of Heaven and called for a general meeting. There were three tribes in Heaven--the tribe of Angels, the tribe of Lucifer, and the new tribe of Mankind. God said, "I have created all of you, and I know your inner selves very well. I just created a new tribe, and I prefer this one over the rest of you, for I put in them some of My divinity, and I took dirt from every part of the earth and mixed it to create such marvelous beings. Moreover, I have given them the choice of both worlds: either to be divine and be close to Me, or not divine and be close to Lucifer. This is why I preferred them over all of you, because I programmed all of you to be divine only. I want all of you to salute Adam and Eve as newly created creatures, and my favorite ones."

The angels stood up and saluted them, but Lucifer stood up and said, "My Almighty God, we will never salute them, because You created them from dirt, and we are created from fire. And fire is far better than dirt." They presented God with a serious case of discrimination and jealousy. This is why jealousy is very destructive, and since then has become prevalent among humans.

God said, "I order you to salute Adam and Eve."

The tribe of Lucifer replied, "Our Almighty God, we really feel that we are better than they are. We will prove that to You; we will have control over them by enticing them and making them follow their destructive natures. Almighty God, will You please give us the opportunity to work with this new tribe of mankind? We will seduce them and show You that humans are false and are not true, even to themselves. Basically, they are worthless beings, and we will show You that when the Day of Judgment comes." They begged God to give them until Judgment Day to show everyone who will be a worthwhile creature.

God granted the Lucifer tribe the new privileges. Then God, who has all the mercy and love for the new creatures, asked for a private meeting with Adam and Eve without the involvement of others. God said, "Listen carefully. I created you and preferred you over all other creatures, but I need to warn you that my intention when I created you was for you to be around Me in Heaven and not to leave my sight. You are my favorites. However, there is now a strong caveat: the devil tribe, (formerly Lucifer but the name was changed because of his disobedience of God), is intending to seduce you and make your lives miserable; that can happen by disobeying Me. If you do that, you will be out of Paradise, you will be disgraced, and you will suffer eternally. God repeated the message and asked, "Are you clear and aware of the danger that surrounds you, and that you will face serious attempts of seduction?"

"Of course," they replied. "We will obey You in whatever You order us to do."

God continued, "Then I will put you to the test and find out. Try to eat from all these trees, but do not eat the fruit of the pomegranate. Please, do not fail the test; I am warning you."

Adam and Eve said, "No, we are confident that we like it here and love the privileges that You have granted us."

God repeated, "Eat from all the fruits and everything that I created for you, except for this tree. Please, do not even get close to it."

They said, "The message is very clear."

And God said, "If you do it, the consequences will be beyond what you can imagine, and can be detrimental." Then God continued, "Listen well. The devil tribe is your enemy, and they will try to seduce you and suggest to you to take the wrong actions. Try not to listen to them at all."

They replied, "Our Almighty God, we are not that stupid to lose all these privileges. We will never fail Your trust in us." They kept wandering around Heaven, enjoying everything that God gave them. The devil tribe watched Adam and Eve carefully and planned to seduce them by any means. The devil tribe was very conniving, sly, and manipulative by nature.

The couple continued to enjoy their new life, discovering everything in Heaven, and sampling all the fruits and vegetables. However, the other tribes noticed a marked change in Adam's behavior since Eve came into his life and wondered what she had brought to change his life. It seemed to the rest of Heaven's inhabitants that Adam tended to act weak and "funny" around her, and sometimes he even lost the essence of his personality. The devil tribe knew the reason and told the rest of Heaven's inhabitants that she captivated him by her vagina. "What is that?" they asked.

The devil tribe explained, "A vagina is an organ in Eve's body that is considered to be the source of all pleasure in the entire universe." Of course, the Angel tribe was not familiar with such a pleasure, but the devil tribe knew it well.

After seven days, the devil went to Adam and Eve and said, "Try to eat from this tree."

They said, "Our Almighty God said, 'Do not even touch it.'"

The devil said, "The reason God prevents you from eating from it is, if you eat from this tree, you will live forever and have all of Heaven for you alone."

The greedy desire started to work in Adam and Eve. Then the devil said, "Listen well. God is not around, and you can eat right now." Of course, because of their naiveté, they were not aware that God sees everything.

Adam was hesitating, so the devil asked Eve, "Why is he that way?"

She said, "I will talk to him. He will do anything now just to please me, as he is lusting for my vagina, even though he might lose his soul for that." The devil observed that Eve had serious influence over the poor creature Adam. She asked him to eat, and both of them ate from the forbidden tree. However, both of them were naïve and inexperienced in how they managed their desires, and curiosity brought them closer to the suggestion of the devil.

Suddenly, the tree's leaves started to fall down over them, and there was a noise in Heaven. The couple felt terrible! God spoke. "Why did you do that? I warned you the devil will try to seduce you. I warned you strongly, but eventually you ate from the forbidden tree. You did not wait even seven days. I am very disappointed in you. I gave you privileges, and that was not enough for you. I am surprised at how much greed you have. And you are now defiant of my order. My judgment is that you go down to the earth."

They asked, "God, what is earth?"

God said, "Earth is a place where you will suffer, you will be the enemy of each other, you will see the cruelty of each other, and you will experience the injustice that you will inflict on each other." Then God continued, "However, there will be another chance for you to come back again to Heaven.

They asked, "How can that be?"

God said, "If you try to follow my instructions and live by the manual which I will have for you, you will come back to Heaven, and you will live here forever. But, if you disobey my earthly instructions, you will go to a different place called Hell, which you have not yet seen."

God has expelled them to earth, and they started a new life on the planet. They gave birth to two sons, Cain and Abel. Then these brothers started to feel jealous of each other. Cain said to Abel, "I do not want to share the earth with you."

Abel said, "Brother, it is large enough for both of us, and more."

"No. I feel I want to kill you," replied Cain. I want to remove you.

Abel said, "I will not participate in that."

Then, one day while Abel sleeping, Cain smashed Abel's head with a big rock, and Abel died. Cain did not even know how to bury him in the ground, so God sent the crow to teach him how to bury his brother. Then Cain felt miserable and regretted that he had killed his brother, but it did not matter because he was a murderer now, by the law of God.

He went about his normal life. He got married and multiplied and populated the earth with his offspring. We have come from our father, Cain, the murderer. Thus, we carry the genes of aggression and murder. The painful fact is that Adam's family was a very dysfunctional and chaotic family. This is why we inherited all our dysfunction from them, and when we see destruction on earth, it is a result of these events from the beginning of the universe.

Adam and Eve expressed sorrow and grief, but their expulsion from the Garden of Eden typified the spiritual fall from their heavenly state of mind to a carnal-minded state. This was the spiritual death of the first humans. That was the start of human misery, and has since played an important role in human's lives.

Almighty God began to watch and see the chaotic world of humans and said, "I do not want to leave them hurting each other, so I will send people to teach them the basic rules of living peacefully with each other. Thus, God sent many prophets to teach people how to be humane with each other. Some of the prophets failed, some succeeded, and some were killed. People did not want to accept them and did not want to see a change. God sent numerous prophets to teach, to warn people and to deliver the message that God wanted to bring them back to Heaven. God's message was clear: life on the earth is a temporary one, and the eternal life is in Heaven next to Him.

But, mankind has refused all the rational arguments of God and has preferred to just be on the earth, enjoying the limited time that we have here. Man has gone too far in his brutality and savagery toward one another, has shed a lot of blood, has committed the most horrible crimes, and destroyed the planet without regard. God is watching us and feels, I'm sure, that He never intended such brutality from His creatures.

The psychological observations of the Adam and Eve story indicate several conclusions. First, Adam and Eve had a defiant nature, even when it was detrimental to their own good. Secondly, Adam felt lonely and wanted to have a companion. His heart yearned for a union with something beyond himself, so God created Eve. She was his salvation. This is why he tended to lose his personal strength when Eve was around him. Third, Eve had tremendous power over Adam, and he had no power over her because he tended to be a slave to her vagina, the seat of ultimate pleasure. He tended to act strangely around her, and sometimes he became hostile just to prove that he was a man. Fourth, greed is a prime motivation for his behavior. Fifth, mankind is very shortsighted and does not look far ahead when it comes to personal greed. Sixth, aggression is embedded in the nature of man, and he does not know how to channel it, or put it to a positive use. Seventh, Adam and Eve were also impatient and did not allow enough time to find out why God prevented them from eating from that specific tree.

So, why did God send prophets into the world? The answer is simple. God considers this life on earth a temporary one and it can be lived as a rehearsal for eternal life in Heaven. There is a sifting process which takes place during this limited life on earth, to separate good people from bad people. The bad will pay a heavy price, and will go to Hell; the consequences are not romantic ones. At the same time, the good ones will be very well rewarded and live through eternity in peace and joy next to God.

Conclusions: Mankind is fabulously stupid because we prefer immediate satisfaction over long-term fulfillment. We are driven by irrational thoughts and inner fears, even though God has clearly shown us the way, and has assured us that if we follow the path He has designed for us, we will gain eternal life. If we follow the path of short pleasure or desire, we will lose. Mankind has chosen the path of losing over the path of gaining. Mankind has chosen the path of hate over the path of love (the path of love is the God pathway). Moreover, mankind's selfishness has destroyed the universe and generated wars, starvation, disease, and injustice. Our earth "has enough for human needs, but not enough for man's greed," as Gandhi put it.

Almighty God showed wisdom when He wove two opposing forces into the fabric of man, both good and bad, to give man the ability to differentiate, the freedom to manifest his humanity and to animate his life, rather than live the stoic life of the angel or the lustful life of the devil. Man has the power to choose, and transcend. When Adam and Eve descended from Heaven down to earth, God specifically asked them to make the earth like Heaven. Unfortunately, their offspring have unconsciously inherited their dysfunctions. The dysfunctional qualities are manifested as greed, aggression, envy, jealousy, poor self-control, selfishness, lust, and hostility. However, they have also inherited the benevolent qualities of love, kindness, compassion, creativity, and the motivation to build.

It seems obvious that the dysfunctional qualities of mankind are the prevailing ones. This is why we have to be mindful that one day we will leave this short life of ours, and the challenge is that we leave the earth in a better condition than when we arrived.

Chapter Two

Is That Part of Human Nature?

Working with people as a psychologist and seeing them for psychotherapy for more than 30 years in different cultures has given me in-depth perspectives regarding human nature. As a result I have developed three perspectives about people's behavior and attitudes.

The First Perspective

Often, people tend to seek their misery, not their happiness, even though the common belief is that people seek their happiness. That is not true, and is a figment of our imaginations. Look around you; you do not need to be a scientist in human behavior to see how many people are happy and joyful. The majority of us are miserable beings, whether we are rich or poor, educated or illiterate, rulers or followers. It does not make any difference. The highest percentages of people are not happy. As the brilliant American actor Woody Allen put it, "people are of two kinds: either miserable or horrible beings.

You may ask "Do you really mean it?" I will say "yes." And the second question you may ask is "Why?" There are some reasons that drove me to come up with such conclusions, as well as how the evolution of psychology has contributed to such views:

1. Our ancestors lived very harsh lives for millions and millions of years, and they encountered many of Nature's troubles – earthquakes, cold, harsh winters, the heat of the desert; animals that ate them, lack of food, wars over natural resources, diseases, and many other hardships. All these experiences are indelible in our conscious mind, and we tend to inherit these experiences from generation to generation, or as Carl Jung called it, the Archetypes. It is the by-product of our experiences, or our existence on the face of the earth, that those experiences shaped us to be gloomy, pessimistic, and illogical beings, whether we like it or not. There are archetypes buried beneath our level of awareness; it is within our collective consciousness.

2. Physically, we are a very fragile people. Illness can very easily overcome us and leave us feeling helpless. We are aware of our fragile nature. A tiny bacteria or virus can paralyze us in a second, and that can feed into our brittle nature. Needless to say, this is not a romantic view of mankind. This view constantly reminds us through a feeling of insecurity and a predictable sense of mortality.

3. We live among uncultivated people, who are jealous and envious by nature, and when they see you happy or well, they tend to you some of their personal disturbance at you. Hence, the majority of us tend to internalize such disturbance, hiding them from others and acting accordingly. That can take away all the joy from life. As John-Paul Sartre said, "hell...is others".

4. Human beings tend to have self-pity, which gives us psychological comfort. Then, when people around us pity us as well, that may give us a sense of weakness. The act of being weak does not make us happy, and thus contributes to our gloomy view of the world around us.

5. There is pleasure in pain. This concept can be attributed to the psychoanalytic theory that an individual tends to derive joy from pain. We call those people masochists; however, almost every one of us has some masochistic tendencies. This means that we inflict either psychological or physical pain on ourselves. Again, Freud called it the pleasure in pain. It also contributes to our negative view of the world around us.

6. As individuals, we come into this world out of the pleasure of two people, who in most instances either have no love for each other, or do not understand the meaning of having a child. Then, we become aware of the complexities in the relationship between our parents, and develop a dislike for ourselves. Often, we come from parents who have no clues in how to rear a child, and they tend to recycle the mistakes they learned from their own parents. Parents can play incredible roles in shaping our psychology, or shaping our perceptions about ourselves. Basically, they draw for us the blueprint that guides us throughout our lives. If our parents are ignorant of how to be parents, they instill in us all manner of pathologies and neuroses. They are the cornerstone in building either a healthy personality, or a disturbed personality. Their contribution to our misery or happiness is very profound.

The Second Perspective

People tend to seek illness and avoid health, for to be physically healthy can be a very challenging and overwhelming task. It is required that an individual know the rules of basic health. Schools do not teach us how to be physically healthy, let alone how to be psychologically healthy. So, people have no knowledge in this area. Being healthy is a full-time job, and the majority of us are fabulously lazy. For example, many people do not brush their teeth after eating a meal. Bacteria can then attack as long as there is some food left in the mouth. This is a simple fact of hygiene.

But what about eating the right food? Normally, we do not obtain knowledge regarding what to eat. Foods tend to be divided into several feuding families. The family of protein tends to dislike the family of carbohydrates; the family of fruits tends to disagree with the family of protein. But, we tend to mix all kinds of food together, and then we have serious health problems. The majority of people over 50 may have serious health concerns because they are putting the wrong fuel into their bodies. Diabetes, high blood pressure, high cholesterol, and acid in the stomach are just a few of the diseases that result from the wrong fuel being put into the body.

The feeling of being sick originates in the early years of life. When we were children, we received attention if we got sick. Sometimes, we even faked it just to get our parents' love and attention. That feeling can stay within us into adulthood as we seek attention for the wrong reasons. This manifests as an extreme case of hypochondria.

Overall, we do not adhere to the rules of health. For example, how many people who are diabetic follow a food schedule? They eat the wrong food; even though they know that it can cause great damage to their health; they do it anyway. There are numerous examples of sick people who do not take charge of their health. Freud clearly indicated that each of us has a strong death wish. We see ourselves indulge in many health risks. Therefore, we may conclude that we, as human beings, tend to avoid health and become ill without being aware of it. Sometimes, though, we are very aware of such health troubles. For example, look around you and see the epidemic of obesity in the world. People try to kill themselves with their teeth. As they say, it is not what *you eat*, it is what *eats you*.

The Third Perspective

As a people, we tend to run away from freedom and seek enslavement. You may say this is not true; we love freedom. Reality gives us a concrete example of our fascination with creating shackles for ourselves.

Our ancestors lived very free lives for millions of years, but modern man has created his own shackles. People used to roam around from land to land without any passport, or boundaries, or even police control. Look what we have done to ourselves; we confine ourselves to one small country and, if we want to travel, we have to have a proper document. That is just one example of losing our freedom.

We used to manage our life without computer systems. Our ancestors lived millions of years without computers, and they did well. Imagine now, if the computer system stopped. Our lives would basically be paralyzed. That is not freedom; we are slaves to the machine. Some say computer usage is an advancement. It can be, but also at the expense of our freedom.

In addition, we also used to be free of any kind of commitment to marriage. Then, humans invented the institution of marriage, and man and woman became slaves to each other. (Please, do not mistake me in this. I am just trying to illustrate examples of our previously free life.)

Erich Fromm wrote a book called *Escape from Freedom* in which he clearly showed that human beings have imprisoned themselves in small boxes and have given it a different and fancy name: nationality. People may call it "love of land" but that is the ultimate in stupidity – that people would attach themselves to a piece of land. It happened accidentally that you were born in Germany, or in the Philippines, or in Brazil. Why identify yourself with a country you never chose? Politicians convince us that we have to fight for our land. No one in the world owns any land. We just come to the earth, live here, and die. Then, other people come to live and die, and that is the natural law. This will be explored further in the following chapters.

Another part of our enslavement is the psychological shackles that our mind has manufactured for us, creating fear. This is detrimental to our inner peace and creativity. For example, we consider our present time a time of anxiety. Our mind has forged a maniacal state. Anxiety has imprisoned and paralyzed us. Fears dominate our thinking and our attitudes, whether these fears are real or imagined. Guess what? Ninety percent of our fears are imagined. Thus, we are not free internally or externally.

With freedom, there is a responsibility, and we run away from such responsibility. It is tempting to delegate our responsibility to others and let them lead our lives. How many people around us give up their freedom and let others manage their lives? That, truly, is the ultimate in human stupidity.

In other parts of the world such as the Middle East, they have another kind of shackle: the cult of personality. The populace overvalues, admires, or even worships those who have power or money. The person who follows a leader is not a free individual, because that person has a sheep mentality. Ironically the majority of us like to follow, not to lead. It is safer and less challenging to follow.

Freedom also requires emotional maturity. The sad fact is, we are not mature enough to conduct or manage ourselves. Thus, we let others do it for us. As a result of our collective attitudes, we are less free, less happy, and more irrational in managing our lives.

Chapter Three

The Psychology of Religion

Man has been living on the earth for eons and innately likes to worship anything considered to have power over his survival, or beyond his visible/invisible world. For example, people have worshipped the stars, moon, sun, thunder, animals, rocks, and have even made a god out of stone and worshipped it. Man has a strong desire to control things around him and to attempt to assign a power to the things that he cannot control so he can feel safe. Since descended from heaven, we are very insecure and find the earth a scary and hostile place.

This is why humans are in a constant search for something beyond the self to worship, or to find meaning for our existence. Moreover, the fear of death has also been a major force in making man insecure, and it tends to get worse when we are faced with drought, thunder, earthquake, or even animal attack. The Immortality has sent a shiver through man's psyche. Thus, it is part of the human psyche to seek a power beyond our comprehension, like Almighty God, so we can deal with immortality. Undoubtedly, that alleviates some of our anxiety and fear. But, man is not rational when it comes to seeking a power outside of himself. Thus, he went even further to sculpt a piece of stone, designated a magical power to it, and then put it in his home to worship. This practice has continued to the present.

The Almighty God saw man's strong desire and struggle to worship something, so He sent prophets to deliver messages to the people and guide them, leading them out of the spiritual darkness and the confusion in which they lived. Of course, each prophet came with a book and a clear message which he delivered to a specific people. For example, Moses (peace be upon Him) came with the message of Judaism; Jesus (peace be upon Him) came with Christianity; and the Prophet Mohammad (peace be upon Him) came with Islam. There were thousands and thousands of prophets who came with different messages, and no doubt God sent them to specific troubled spots to help. Ironically, most of the prophets came to the Arabs and the Jews. History has informed us only about the recent prophets; they were all male, and I do not know why.

Each prophet brought a message that was a continuation of the previous prophet. For example, Prophet Mohammad (peace be upon Him) came to the Arabs because they used to live in total ignorance and spiritual darkness, manifested in burying woman alive, tribal pride, slavery, injustice, domination of certain classes of people, and all manner of abuse to each other.

The message from God was loud and clear: the inhabitants of the earth must try to be peaceful, helpful, try to live in harmony and love one another. That was the predominant message from all the prophets throughout history.

Humans took those messages from God and applied their own interpretations and perceptions to them. Most of the time man twisted the original messages from God and structured them according to his own malicious purposes, desires, and wishes. For example, in the mid-1800s, the Church of Europe issued a decree that buying and selling black people as slaves was allowed, in the Christian view. Also, there are numerous examples today regarding the killing of innocent people in the name of Islam. Mankind has written his own scriptures to suit his own wicked perceptions about the world around him. God has kept sending messengers to warn people that if they did not obey the instructions of God, God would punish them severely. Unfortunately, mankind has never listened to these warnings, but arrogantly has defied the order of God.

For example, when Noah was sent by God to his people, asking them to be kind and just to each other, they laughed at him and never believed him. Then God instructed him to build the ark, and Noah asked the people over and over to obey God, and warned if they did not, the earth would be flooded. Again, they did not listen. Then God began to flood the earth. Even Noah's own son did not believe him. He saw the rain coming and the earth beginning to flood. Noah asked his son to get into the ark, but he said, "No, I will go to the mountain and save myself."

Noah said, "Son, I am a prophet, and God will not stop the rain, and it will cover the mountaintop and the whole earth. Why do you want to lose your life? Please, son, get in the ark."

His son said, "No, I do not want to," and disappointed his father. Then, he drowned.

It seems that the irrational and defiant nature of mankind is embedded in the fabric of our psyche. God, with great mercy, warned man that this life is a temporary one, a mere rehearsal for the eternal one. God indicated in his holy books, "I have put you to the test," and you must try to pass the test so you can live forever next to God in paradise. But, the nature of man is to be impatient and to want immediate gratification over long-term fulfillment. Almighty God became fed up and decided "enough" and vowed to send no more prophets until the Judgment Day. Man does not know the purpose of his existence, and he has followed the wicked motive in himself.

Often, religion becomes a source of serious conflict, and it has been associated with some of the most horrific crimes ever committed on the face of the earth. There has been a lot of bloodshed in the name of religion. People are very dogmatic when it comes to religion. One person may say, "I know the way," and force his way on others. And if others do not follow his way, he may kill them to "save them from Hell", in his eyes. We have become totally blind and have no regard for human values. It is the saddest reality of the human condition that religion has become a tool for revenge, for abuse, and for ultimate cruelty. Of course, the teachings of religion are very far from all of that, but when human malevolent intent prevails, then the ugly face of humanity appears.

If we look closely at any religion, we may find that it consists of three pillars: faith, conduct and ritual. All these components are clearly spelled out in the books of God. The faith component is the most important one according to God's message. The second one mentioned is the conduct, or the behavioral component, and how people carry and manage themselves in the world around them. Finally, the third component is ritual, which seems the most prevalent one in all religions. Let us take a close look at each one of the components.

The First Pillar: Faith

This pillar believes God is the Almighty power, the Omnipresence, the Omnipotent, the Creator of all living and non-living things in the universe, and beyond our visible world. Once you have faith in the deep recesses of your heart, you have a connection to the ultimate loving power which encompasses the whole world. Having a deep faith can give you the spiritual nourishment that sustains every aspect of your life. Faith is the cornerstone of everything in a person's life. Faith can penetrate your whole being and shine internally as well as radiate outside of you.

People pay lip service to faith, but deep down do not have it, because they are confusing faith with the practicing of rituals. Faith can swell your heart with love for God, for yourself, and for people around you, and it can be the utmost solution to human suffering. The individual with faith does not know fear at all, because love and fear cannot be in the same heart at the same time. This is a very delicate psychological fact that must be understood, because the opposite of love is not hate, but fear.

Having a true faith can make you a sensitive, caring, considerate, and loving human being. Moreover, there is a saying; our anxiety can be measured by how much far we are from God. The closer we are to God, the less anxious that we are.

The Second Pillar: Conduct

Conduct, or behavior, is the second pillar. As is said, "Please do not tell me or preach to me; just show me." Your behavior reflects your religious beliefs as displayed in your attitude and conduct. The teachings of religion are manifested in a person's behavior toward others, carrying himself in a manner in accordance with the welfare of fellow humans. Diabolically, our behavior can be the opposite of what we profess. This is why we see people who are cynical when it comes to religion. We have lost faith in religious people who always shout so loud while their actions do not match their rhetoric. This is called hypocrisy, and it is one of the salient characteristics of the religious preachers.

The Third Pillar: Ritual

Unfortunately, rituals are the most dominant part of all religious practices. People spend inordinate amounts of time and energy practicing all manner of rituals. Often these rituals are devoid of any spiritual fulfillment. Practicing rituals is merely habit, learned in the early years of life. We grow up without even questioning the validity of these rituals. The practice of rituals has exceeded all other pillars of religion, and is not confined to one religion. The time spent in the practice of rituals is immense, and can be at the expense of the pillars of faith and conduct.

Faith requires a fundamental challenge to the core of our soul, while the practice of rituals can be empty. We observed our parents or the people around us and we followed them. Or is it just the mere imitation of others, as a matter of habit? The practice of rituals can serve deep psychological purposes. It may give us certain false satisfactions that we are connected to God (even though our hearts are devoid of faith). Or, we like to be seen by others, just to show off. It may give us certain power, or we may use it to manipulate others, or gain an advantage over others. Faith, on the other hand, is a relationship between only an individual and God, and no one else knows about it.

Conclusion

Humankind has been yearning for a psychological union with the Creator since we were separated, when Adam and Eve committed their defiant act, and God ordered them to leave Paradise. Thus, we are frantically seeking to be reunited again with the omnipotent God. We are wandering aimlessly on the earth, and we have created many gods just to soothe our pain of separation from the main source of life.

All of humanity prays daily to alleviate their suffering. While some suffering is self-inflicted, other suffering is inflicted by fellow humans. In addition, there is suffering that has been inflicted upon us by nature (natural disasters) and because God gets angry with us.

When we are unhappy within ourselves, we tend to lash out at the people around us. Mankind has not been happy for a while. Thus, we tend to wage wars with our fellow humans in the name of religion or nationality or for whatever reason that we might invent. The greatest enemy to man is man himself because we are born with irrational, destructive tendencies. Specifically, I am referring to the male gender, because the female gender differs in its perspective. The female does not like war; she wants to protect her offspring, and they see blood in their monthly menstruation. The male, on the other hand, wants to see blood in war. Religious teachings try to put a cap on this tendency.

Religions have collectively failed to correct the nature of mankind. Religion may score some success in very limited areas. However, the focus of religion has shifted since its inception merely to practice rituals. That can be simply a performance of a mechanical act, mostly void of any meaning that could bring true change to the yearning heart of man. The heart of man is still filled with fear, anxiety, worry, and greed, because the focus is not on purifying his soul, but rather on greed and self-centeredness. This is one reason why the majority of the populations of the world suffer from a shortage of food, from disease, and, most of all, from depression.

Thus, the ultimate solution for human dilemmas, as far as religion is concerned, is to cultivate our hearts and souls with true faith, compassion and love. That allows us to be happy and to share what we have with our fellow man.

The following chapter examines closely why religion became the source of our disappointment, suffering, agony and disturbances. We will explore dogma and how it has brought us all types of pain, because religions are a very essential part of daily human psyche.

Chapter Four

The Tyranny of Religious Dogma

Dogma: When you believe that your faith or your religion is the correct one, your path is the only one, your way is better than the rest, your teaching is the superior one, and your prophet is the answer to the rest. In other words, you believe the dogma of your religion has the answer to the human condition. Once any individual has such a belief, he will stimulate other groups from different religions to become defensive and protective toward their religions. Such attitudes plant the seeds of destruction, and the chasm among religious believers thus widens. People become apprehensive about their religion and try to arm themselves, so to speak, against a supposed or imagined enemy.

Thus, religious dogma is the main cause of human conflict and suffering, while ironically, the message of God in all religions is tolerance and love for each other, whether Muslim or Christian, Jewish or Hindu, Buddhist, or even non-believers. So how has religious dogma developed to the degree that we are unable to contain? We are paying a very high cost with human lives, almost daily throughout the world.

Religion is a very essential and indispensable part of our lives, even though it brought disastrous consequences to the human community. Please do not take me wrong. I am talking here about our distorted interpretations of the message that came from Almighty God. God sent numerous prophets, and the message was very clear: human beings have the potential to be good, as well as the potential to be evil. Thus, God in his messages tackled the evil tendency within us. But reality is the wonderful message of Ibrahim, Jesus, Moses and Mohammad (peace be upon Them) has been reduced to empty rituals that have kept people from knowing the true message of God. In other words, people have not translated the wonderful message of Almighty God into real action and attitudes in their daily lives.

Why most of the prophets came to the Arabs and Jews. Can we really examine and have the courage to ask why Almighty God has sent numerous prophets to Arabs and Jews, yet they were not the only population inhabiting the earth at that time. By their nature, Arabs and Jews are defiant, difficult people to manage. Somehow, the words of God have not penetrated their souls. It has been argued that God sent his prophets to them because they are the chosen people. It is true, they are a chosen people because they are difficult and defiant, and normally God's messages come to people who need change. Either they are weak and oppressed, or merely people with evil inclinations. Thus, God wants to salvage them from evil forces that have possessed them for a long time.

We are wonderful in performing and adhering to the empty rituals, but God sent religions to structure our lives. Unfortunately, the focus became the religions themselves, not the connection with Almighty God. Those are different concepts. Humans are corrupted spiritually. We need no evidence of that, as the human condition is manifested in wars, killing, abuses, hatred, envy, jealousy, discrimination, worship of money, and on and on.

Religious dogma. Religion itself is wonderful, but when it comes to dogma, the danger lies within. Dogma says "my religion is better and the right one, and if you do not follow me, then you should be eliminated." Believe in that, and we like to recruit people to join our religion, and we do not leave people alone. Why? If you are insecure about your religion, you need more people to substantiate your beliefs, so you can feel good about yourself. The more who join my religion, the more secure you become. That gives a sense of collective power. Of course, it is a false perception, but somehow, our sly minds want us to believe it.

The other thing that contributes to this mindset is the absence of love from religious teachings. God's message in itself is love, but we are not mature enough to fathom such a concept. Or, we love the people who believe in the same faith we have, and of course we hate people who do not hold our beliefs. Therefore, it is better to eliminate them, because to us they represent evil forces. Human history has witnessed incredible atrocities and heinous crimes in the name of religion; the Crusaders are an example of that atrocity and brutality. Each person feels they are fighting evil: people who have beliefs different than ours.

Eric Fromm said love is the only sane and satisfactory answer to the problem of human nature. The message of God is love, but the dark soul of humans is incapable of internalizing the love of God. We may say it verbally, and we may preach it to millions, but it is merely empty rhetoric. It does not translate to action, behavior, or attitudes.

If we really examine the core of human satisfaction and fulfillment, we discover that we all, without exception, yearn to love and be loved. But there is a paradox here. Since birth, we seek love from our parents or any other care givers. Some are fortunate enough to receive it, but the majority of us do not. So, we grow up as beggars for love. We create all kinds of scenarios to obtain love, and often these scenarios fail. We get hurt and heartbroken on the individual level. As societies, we take advantage of each other, and rarely have mercy in our hearts for fellow humans.

This negative picture of the human condition was drawn by God. The Creator drew it when Adam and Eve disobeyed the order of God. (I will have a serious conversation with Adam on the day of Judgment, and ask why in the world out of the millions and millions of trees, he went straight to the tree that God ordered him not to eat from? Adam caused all the troubles and pain on the earth.) There was no excuse for Adam to disobey God, no matter what the justification. God gave him free will, and his free will brought him to disobey God. There is only one reason for that: his evil tendency. We inherited that. It is in our genes to be defiant and foolish people. (*Mean Genes*, Terry Burnham and Jay Phelan, 2000)

The best example of this was when Noah constructed the Ark, and the only people who boarded were the good, pure believers. After the flood, supposedly the earth should have had no evil, because all who were in the ark were good, and the bad were drowned. The puzzling question is, why was the earth again populated with evil, malicious people? The only answer is the evil tendency within all of us. We inherited it, because it was instilled within man since the beginning of the universe. Adam and Eve had it and it has come to us through their genes.

The humanistic psychology movement argues that we are born to be natural. That is incorrect; we are born with the basic human tendencies: aggression, selfishness, greed, mediocrity and laziness. God in His books indicated that clearly, as well as the psychology of individuality. Human history has given us clear proof of that.

Now we are left with a serious human dilemma. Which religions are supposed to find a solution, and cultivate our corrupted nature? We have failed miserably at translating the teachings of God into real actions and attitudes. We instead have used religions as a means of control, to subject each other to inordinate abuse and brutality. As a result, man alienates himself from himself, and from others. He becomes desensitized to the suffering of fellow humans. His soul is barren, and he strives for power and control. At the bottom of his soul he wants to control his fellow humans, and if opportunity permits, he will not hesitate a minute to abuse others. This is just to satisfy his evil tendency, which religion came to cultivate, and put his corrupted soul under its control.

It seems there is no solution to religious dogma, or the dilemma of cruelty and inhuman treatment of man by his fellow man, in the name of religion. Someday, God may bring some miracle, to take us away and cleanse us to remove the dark spots in our souls, or replace us with others. But even so, we would mainly see the same situation all over again, because of our corrupt soul, or our "mean genes". We did not have a choice to come to earth, because Adam and Eve made the ultimate mistake, and God had no option but to evict them from Paradise. We came to earth and were not mature enough to manage our lives. Perhaps, our souls have not evolved to the level that we can be with each other and live harmoniously. Thus, all the dysfunctions which prevail in our daily lives.

Although there are some thinkers who believe religious faith is not necessarily to liberate our corrupt souls, it does assist in the process. What else can liberate our corrupt souls, and set us free from malicious intent? Plato's concept in his *Republic,* was society should be governed by philosophers, thinkers and intellectuals, because they adhere to universal moral and ethical standards of what is good for individuals and society. Another solution to our corrupt souls is to rear our children with very strict moral standards, and design curriculums which to not cultivate evil tendencies within us, so we can share our lives on earth without the pain or suffering which we tend to inflict on each other.

Chapter Five

The Paradigm of the Seven Deadly Enemies

Summary concepts. Since we were embryos, we have been genetically programmed for illness, vulnerability, or susceptibility for certain diseases and behavioral propensities. There are a host of things that have been programmed within us, even before we open our eyes. When we are born, we begin a serious struggle with seven deadly enemies. Three are from inside us, and four are external.

The internal enemies are built into our psyche. The first is our **wicked nature**. We are programmed from the start to be wicked and corrupt, or kind and compassionate. The second enemy is the **sly mind**, which is designed to make us unhappy and keep us in constant worry. The third is **illness,** which has three components: autoimmune system diseases, which tend to turn against us and viciously attack us without mercy; germs; and mental illness.

The external enemies start with **our body and its relationship with time**. As the years accumulate our bodies become fragile and frail. Aging takes place, and eventually we deteriorate to the final stage, death. The fifth enemy is **people**. In general, people tend to be the cause of most disturbances. They can inflict damage, psychological or otherwise. The sixth enemy is **mishaps**, which are often caused by natural disasters. We do not know when disasters like earthquakes, car accidents or fires may strike. Mishaps can be anything that happens without any obvious reason. The seventh enemy is the **invisible forces** that attack us. We call it the **Jinn**, or evil forces.

From the moment we come into the world until we depart to our eternal life, we struggle with these deadly enemies. The fact is, we have no control over these enemies; we are helpless in the face of such challenges. Thus our life is filled with pain and suffering, only sometimes punctuated by moments of joy and happiness.

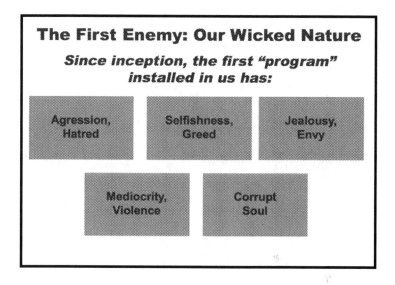

The first deadly enemy: our wicked nature. When God created us, He instilled in us our wicked nature, which manifests as greed, hatred, selfishness, aggression, mediocrity, envy, jealousy and corruption. But, God also instilled in us a benevolent nature, manifested as kindness, hope, love, compassion, helpfulness and giving. Unfortunately, God started with our wicked nature. That was clearly manifested in the behavior of Adam and Eve. Sadly, their wicked natures superseded benevolent nature; they committed original sin by following their wicked inclinations and defying the order of God. They ate the pomegranate which resulted in our suffering and misery.

The result of this sin was man's expulsion from heaven, and man came to earth. Then a horrible crime was committed by Cain, who killed his brother Abel. This act clearly shows how envy can be devastating to all of us, and is a large factor in human nature. Abel did not have offspring. Therefore, we all came from the murderer, Cain. The start of the universe was a corrupt one, and we have struggled with it since. This first deadly enemy was the installation of our wicked nature, prior to being given the good nature.

Even at birth, we are already programmed to do wicked things. But there are two "programs" that are "installed" in us. Just like a computer, what you get out depends on what you put in. Although the first program is wickedness and corruption, the second one is kindness and compassion. We spend our lives struggling with those two factions.

The wicked takes over in most instances, and the benevolent in fewer. Our beginning was inherently bad, so the wicked side has worked against us since conception. Therefore our life is heavy with struggles to fight our wicked nature. Scientific research support this hypothesis, as well as religions also support it unequivocally, and the majority of people on earth have a strong belief in religion.

We are doomed from the start by our wicked nature; it is our deadly enemy. It is always tempting us to do detrimental things. It also stimulates us to violate others and take advantage of them, even among family members. That, unfortunately, is human nature. It's not a romanticized idea of our nature, it is reality. We appear helpless in the face of such wickedness. No matter how much we try to suppress our wicked nature, it often manifests by surprise and rears its ugly head, and asserts its existence in spite of our rejection of it. Some in the Sufi division of Islam realize the danger of our corrupt nature, and they are dedicated to suppress our greedy, selfish, and aggressive nature.

Why did Almighty God, the merciful and compassionate, instill us with a wicked nature, and then left us to struggle with it? I have no answer, and I believe our whole existence is still a mystery, let alone knowing the wisdom of being created with a corrupted nature. I have a strong belief that God is just, but as human beings we have a very limited understanding of the nature of the universe, and we do not understand why things are the way they are.

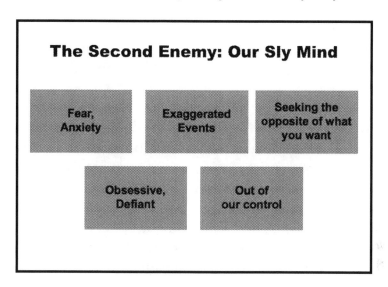

The second deadly enemy: the **sly mind**. If we investigate the nature of the mind, it becomes apparent that it is designed for life in the jungle, not for modern times. Our ancestors lived very harsh, brutal lives. Thus, our brain reacts to a simple threat as serious and detrimental, and sometimes our mind depicts a distant problem and exaggerates it. Often the mind fabricates problems which don't really exist, just to protect us.

Metaphorically speaking, if you have a serious conversation with your mind and ask, "Why do you do that to me, and make my life a living hell?" the mind will answer, "It makes sense to me; I am here just to protect you." And when you tell your mind, "We are not living in the jungle; we are living with air conditioning. No animals are around to devour us. So please, just relax and take it easy." The answer will be, "No, I am not structured to function that way. My job is not to make you happy; my job is to protect you, even at the expense of your happiness."

Sometimes the mind acts like a magnet with its poles reversed. It attracts what we hope to avoid and repels that which we desire.

(Shawn Smith, 2011). Smith also indicated in his book, *The Human Mind*, that "we are wired for a simpler and more hostile world, where small problems had big consequences. For the most part, humans no longer need to worry about starving, freezing, or being eaten by predators, but our mind, which evolved facing life and death decisions on the savanna, may not have received the memo."

Ironically, the more we attempt to control bothersome thoughts, the stronger they become, and that increases our problems. For example, if you keep thinking about something you do not want, you will get exactly that thing. Our mind never stops the chatter, even when we go to sleep. Our mind always tries to fish for problems, even if we are not in danger. It never rests until it finds some sort of problem. It is like a dog which barks all the time. The dog may hear someone walking on the next street, but the dog thinks there is danger and keeps barking. Our mind smells a problem from a distance and tries to exaggerate it, even if the problem is minute. That is what turns our lives into constant worry and fear.

The old wisdom indicates, "do not believe everything you think", because our mind is overprotective of us. Our mind is a voracious machine that keeps fears and worries for a long time, and pushes them to the forefront occasionally, mainly when we just feel a little happy. It's as if our mind wants to tell us, "I am not here to make you happy," and it seems that you forget your worries, so the mind keeps bringing the worry to the foreground over and over, just to disturb us. The mind has a skewed view of the world. We are often jolted by a danger which does not exist at that moment. But, our mind tends to fish for remote problems as if it wants to do a favor for us. In reality, the mind is messing up our lives, and making them a living hell.

The other salient characteristic of the sly mind is it tends to see the flaws in situations and to anticipate undesirable outcomes. This is ubiquitous among human minds. Another name for this is "pessimistic thinking"; it seems we are wired to notice problems. What necessitates such torment? The mind is prone to detect danger even when danger is unlikely to exist. One serious example of such torment is OCD – Obsessive/Compulsive Disorder – in which a person can feel the battle raging within, and nothing is rational about it. Our minds may see something we do not see. Thus, we must not trust our perception of things. We may perceive the world as stable and predictable, when in fact the information percolating through the mind and into our consciousness frequently offers a skewed view of things around us. Thus, our mind is really the main enemy that we carry with us from birth to death. Animals are born with instincts, and humans are born with a brain. Are animals better than we are, or are we better than they are? I do not know the answer; perhaps you have some perspective over the tragic nature of the mind.

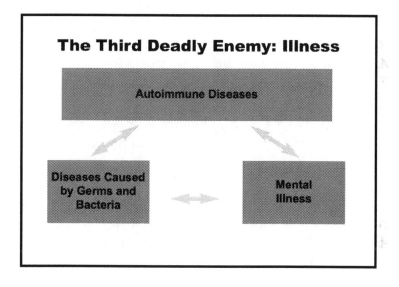

The third deadly enemy: illness. This enemy can be divided into three parts which attack and cause illness to our bodies and minds. First is the attack by our **autoimmune system**, and is internal. Second is the attack by **viruses and bacteria** and is external. Finally, there is **mental illness**, which is brain malfunction.

Illness, Part 1: Autoimmune diseases. The autoimmune system is designed to protect us. But occasionally it turns against us and attacks us with a vengeance. The list of autoimmune diseases caused by such attacks numbers more than 80. These diseases can make life a living hell. Treatments are difficult, and some are not effective. The system attacks our tissues and cells and destroys them; it considers them intruders. Some unfortunate people are infected with such diseases, and they suffer all their lives. Perhaps they are pre-disposed or susceptible to such diseases.

Our immune system is very a complex network of special cells and organs that defends the body from germs and other foreign invaders. At the core of the immune system is the ability to tell the difference between self and non-self, i.e., what is you and what is foreign. Unfortunately, serious flaws happen within the system which can make the body unable to tell the difference between the two. When this happens, the body makes autoantibodies which attack normal cells by mistake, while the T cells fail to do their job of keeping the immune system in line. The result is a misguided attack on your own body. It is unfortunately quite common and can lead to disability or death.

No one is sure what causes autoimmune diseases, but they do run in families and affect women more than men. Autoimmune diseases are the most common cause of all diseases in the world today. It is a deadly enemy, in that our own protective forces start to attack our body. Each disease affects the body in different ways. For instance, the autoimmune reaction is directed against the brain in Multiple Sclerosis, and the gut in Crohn's disease, while Lupus affects tissues and organs.

Autoimmune diseases are chronic and can be life-threatening, and usually last a lifetime. There are more than 80 types, including: Addison's disease, Alopecia areata, hepatitis, inner ear disease, pancreatitis, cardiomyopathy, endometriosis, narcolepsy, peripheral neuropathy, ulcerative colitis, vitiligo, cancer, type 1 diabetes mellitus and rheumatoid arthritis. Sadly enough, this enemy leads individual bodies to self-destruction.

Illness, Part 2: Germs, Viruses and Bacteria. This enemy comes from the external environment. Millions and millions of them are out there. They enter our body and wreak havoc. They take the joy out of our lives. They make us sick, suffer and we could die from this enemy. We appear helpless and hopeless in the face of such an attack. For example, if you have influenza, you will feel basically joyless and hate your life, and become very gloomy.

A **virus** is submicroscopic parasitic particle that infects cells in biological organisms; it is self-producing. Viruses are much smaller than cells; in fact viruses are basically capsules that contain genetic materials, responsible for causing a wide range of diseases, such as the common cold, Ebola fever, influenza, HIV, measles, meningitis, and more. The treatment for these diseases is antiviral medications. When viruses attack the human body, they enter a few cells and control the host cells, producing that part needed to replicate themselves. It's a very sneaky way to operate inside human cells! In the process, the host cells eventually are eradicated. Remember, antibiotics have no effect on viruses.

Bacteria are a major group of living organisms, the most abundant of all organisms, ubiquitous in soil and water. A bacterium is a single cell organism that can only be seen with the aid of a microscope. When infectious bacteria enter the body, the number of bacteria increases and produces powerful chemicals called toxins, which destroy certain cells in the tissues they attack. That is what makes us sick.

However, not all bacteria are harmful. Some like to live in the human body, such as in the gut and mouth. Diseases caused by bacteria can be treated with antibiotics. Bacterial diseases include pneumonia, acne, sore throat, cholera, tuberculosis, and urinary tract infections.

These first two parts, autoimmune diseases and viral/bacterial diseases, are horrible little monsters encroaching on the threshold of life. They are formidable enemies, because they constantly mutate to breach our immune system's defenses. Often, they result in long-term suffering and take all the joy out of life.

Illness, Part 3: Mental illness. According to scientific research, about 11 percent of the world's population suffers from mental illness. We may know what has contributed to it, but some of the illnesses remain a mystery. For example, schizophrenia and paranoia are still unsolved puzzles. The life of the mentally ill person is pure hell to him as well as to his family. Unlike physical illness, which is obvious and for which the treatment can be very successful, mental illness is complicated, very hard to treat and there is almost no cure. Modern medicine has made giant leaps in managing and treating physical illness, but it remains very short of managing mental illness. The mentally ill person lives in constant internal torment, and occasionally can be dangerous to himself and to society.

Mental illness tends to run in a family. Allopathic medicine has many antidepressant, antianxiety, and antipsychotic medications, which help the patient to lead, relatively speaking, a semi-normal life. Mental illness can be devastating to society, and society invests a great deal to treat these people, unsuccessfully. Mental illness can be a deadly enemy to the human soul.

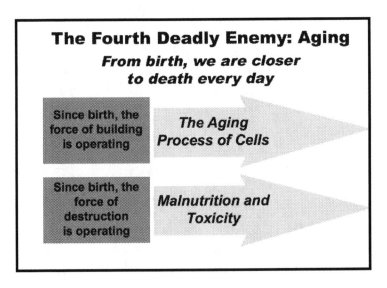

The fourth deadly enemy: the aging process. The minute we are born, there are two forces working within us: the force of building and the force of destruction, or the force of death. Every day, in our bodies, thousands and thousands of cells die and new cells come to life. These processes continue within every single organ of our bodies. In our youth, the process of building is greater than the process of destruction. But around 40, our body starts to go downhill, as more cells die than are created. We lose our youth. While once we were strong and beautiful, now we become weak and aged. We realize what a fleeting and comfortable place youth actually was. As time goes on, our body becomes our worst enemy, and we could become imprisoned in it.

Although it is unlikely we would be attacked by a terrorist, we can be attacked by our heart, and it can kill us. Malfunctions of our organs can become our enemy and launch attacks on us, in addition to the aging process. From birth, we are counting down toward death, and as the years accumulate, the body deteriorates, and we become brittle and frail.

In the aging process, the functions of the body slow down. There is compounding physical decline with aging, and we see serious slowing of functions in every part of the body. In general, muscles, blood vessels, bone and other tissues lose their elasticity. The heart become less efficient, bones become weaker and metabolism slows down. Aging affects every part of the body. Our appearance changes, our vision deteriorates and our eyes become less sensitive to light reception.

Another function affected by aging is hearing. Motor skills also suffer with age. Muscles become weaker, reflexes slow down and flexibility decreases. Our cognitive reaction time also becomes slower; an older person takes longer to process incoming stimuli. Sleep becomes more difficult, and there is confusion and disorientation associated with mild dementia and cognitive degeneration. Aging likely causes us to develop wrinkles and gray hair, and it also affects our teeth and sexuality.

Within the cardiovascular system, as we age our heart rate becomes slightly slower and the heart enlarges. Our blood vessels and arteries become stiffer, causing our heart to work harder to pump blood, which can lead to high blood pressure. Bones, joints and muscles shrink in size and density. Muscles generally lose strength and flexibility and we become less coordinated. The bladder and urinary tract are also affected; men may develop prostate enlargement and woman have menopause. And, unfortunately, our memory becomes less effective with age.

The human body actually goes through one long continuous process of change, from the moment of conception right through to decomposition after death. Until the end of puberty we are still growing and developing into an adult. We then enter a period of many years when the body may not change much and continue to function in a fairly regular way. Then there's a period where more and more physical changes occur that lead to gradual decline in most of our bodily functions. In the third decade the shape of the body typically changes. Studies show the rate of growth of our nails declines gradually from our 20s onward, and the lens of the eye becomes less flexible from our 40s onward.

How do our cells age? As years pass, damage occurs deep within the molecules of the cells. The cells work less efficiently, and the tissues and organs begin to deteriorate and are less able to repair themselves. We know many of our cells, especially our skin or the lining of the gut, are in a constant state of recycling and renewal to replace cells that are lost or worn out. But chromosomes have a limited ability to copy themselves each time a cell divides. The DNA must copy itself but the very ends of the chromosomes -- called telomere -- do not get copied. It is rather like photocopying a page of text and losing the first and the last lines each time. As a result, the telomere and chromosomes get progressively shorter until a critical length is reached and the cell can no longer divide to repair or replace itself. The gradual failure of the cells to repair or replace themselves is the basis of the physical change of aging, and can be found in every organ or tissue of the body. Some are more likely to lead to disease. Thus, the aging process is another deadly enemy that keeps hunting us, and after age 50 we become vulnerable to disease and all manner of malfunctions of the body.

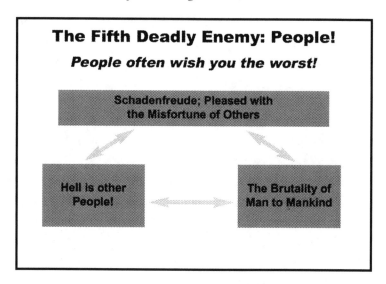

The Fifth Deadly Enemy: People!

People often wish you the worst!

Schadenfreude; Pleased with the Misfortune of Others

Hell is other People!

The Brutality of Man to Mankind

The fifth deadly enemy: people! Jean-Paul Sartre, in his encapsulated wisdom, said that "hell is other people". People tend to inflict a lot of pain on each other, and may even cause serious damage. People in general rarely wish us well. Gore Vidal said, "It is not enough to succeed, others must fail". Why are people pleased with others' misfortune or failures? While there are some people who want the best for us, they are the minority. The majority of people in general do not wish us well. I do not say that hypothetically; it is very clearly stated in the books of God, in which we are described as sinners, wrongdoers and corrupt. All that was begun by Adam and Eve, when they defied the order of God and subjected themselves to temptation. As a result of their horrible mistakes, we were expelled from heaven.

Often, people do not know what is good for them. They are also unhappy with their own makeup, so they tend to lash out at the person closest to them. There is a German word for wishing bad for other people: *Schadenfreude.* It is not uncommon to feel pleasure over the failure of other people, and this German word has become universal in its expression of this feeling. It is a nasty emotion which defines enjoyment obtained from the troubles of others. John Portman investigated this phenomenon of the human impulse of taking a perverse pleasure in others' pain.

We all suffer from dark emotions, and they manifest as malice, cruelty, sadism and humiliation. Professor Smith sees repugnant emotions as a part of human nature; we are programmed to feel that way. They result from envy and resentment, and the people we envy are the people who are around us.

Professor Feather came up with a Social Comparison Theory: people evaluate themselves not by objective standards but by comparison to the people around them. Hilde Spiel sees malice like a game of poker or tennis; you do not play it with anyone who is manifestly inferior to you. Schopenhauer argues that to feel envy is human, but to enjoy other people's misfortune is diabolical.

The major reason for being pleased with the misfortune of another person is this person's misfortune may somehow benefit us. It may, for example, emphasize our superiority, or our belief that people deserve to have such misfortune. Or, perhaps it is a sadistic tendency to derive pleasure from inflicting pain on others. Or we may believe justice has been done for wicked people.

There is a Talmudic saying, "The tasks of the righteous get done by others." This is a kind of unsolicited gift, in which we take delight in the downfall of others, and feel pleasure over the suffering of others. This is why human history is filled with wars, brutality, abuse and suffering. People can be deadly enemies to each other. Thus, we invented war machines to protect ourselves from one another. A close look at the budgets of each country, showing how much they spend in armaments, can send a shiver down the spine. It all boils down to fear of each other, or the wicked desire to hurt each other.

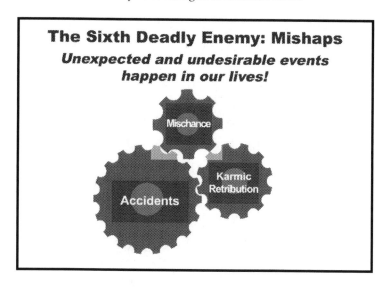

The sixth deadly enemy: mishaps. This enemy is external, and can be defined as unexpected and undesirable events, an unforeseen event, or one without an apparent cause. Or it can be mischance, a misadventure or a casualty like a car accident, injury, fire, or anything over which you have no control. Why do bad things happen to people? Many concepts have attempted to explain that. For instance, the law of Karma, or fate, says as a result of action taken in past lives, it is time for you to pay back what you have done. That is called Karmic retribution for previous transgressions. Or because your thoughts produce your experience in life, negative thoughts cause negative events. Conversely, positive thoughts create positive events.

Why is life often characterized by misfortune, sadness, untimely death and tragedies of all sorts? Bad things happen to all kinds of people. As sources of influence, they can be referenced to such things as the moon, sun, stars and other planetary influence. Adverse events can also be explained as the influence of God or evil, or they may be sheer bad luck. All of these are unexplainable phenomena.

There are also things which have no human involvement, like sickness, genetic miscues, or random natural disasters. Why, we scream at the sky; that is at fault? Who can we blame?

Unfortunately, there are no good answers to that either. Bad things happen through no fault of God or man. But the question remains, are we merely subject to the whims of chance without having control over our lives?

There are three general types of misfortune: the first is those caused by nature unforeseen or impossible to prevent, including wind, rain, ice, snow, lightning, landslides and tectonic events. They contribute to accidents by presenting extreme conditions beyond human capability. The second kind of mishap is material failure or mechanical flaw, which can cause a change in structures and machinery resulting in serious damage or injury. Third, there is human error, usually present to some degree but not necessarily negligence; like crossing the street and being hit by a car.

Laurence Peter said, "Fortune knocks but once, but misfortune has much more patience." Each life has a mixture of fortune and misfortune, pleasant and unpleasant experiences, success and failure. Misfortune can come in many different ways. It may be a serious illness, the loss of a job, failure in a project, a marriage breaking down, or financial bankruptcy, and the saddest misfortune was Boston Marathon that few athletes have lost their legs. Therefore, mishaps or misfortune can be considered a deadly enemy and may cause serious damage to the body, our property, or to loved ones. The most dangerous part of this enemy is that we have no control over it.

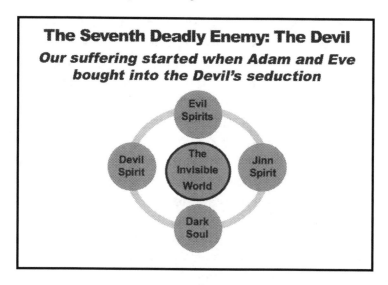

The Seventh Deadly Enemy: The Devil
Our suffering started when Adam and Eve bought into the Devil's seduction

The seventh deadly enemy: evil forces. This enemy is esoteric one, that we are surrounded by Jinn and evil forces. There are two worlds, invisible and visible. It is very easy to understand our visible world through our five senses, but it can be very difficult to understand our invisible world. Our visible world is managed or controlled by the invisible world. Our invisible world is filled with evil forces that can hurt us seriously. Scientific research has been investigating these forces and their influence on humans. As Mario Bunge said, "The trademark of modern culture is science; if you can fake this, you have it made."

How can we have insight into an unknown world that lies beyond the limit of our physical senses? People tend to place foundation upon their own personal experiences; for example, I am hot, I am cold. I saw something I cannot explain. You have heard the saying, "seeing believes", but sometimes believing is seeing; it works both ways. We have to open our minds to things around us we cannot comprehend, and which we cannot see, but which exist.

We cannot actually see the air, but we know it is real, because we can feel it, we cannot see ultraviolet or infrared light or radio signals, but we know they exist in a certain frequency or spectrum. Normally unobservable by human eyes, we can feel the existence of Satan, or the Devil. God's words tell us that our world is filled with evil forces; these forces work against us, and seek to harm us. This has been true since the beginning of creation, when Lucifer enticed our father and mother to follow him. Our Almighty God, upset with them, kicked them out of heaven. That was the start of our suffering. God's words in the Holy Quran and the Holy Bible say that evil forces have the power to deceive us, and that they work consistently to keep us from knowing the truth. God also warns us in numerous verses in His holy books that we have to be aware of these forces and try not to give in to their temptations, which can result in catastrophe in our lives.

The most painful case of evil forces' influence is that of our father and mother, Adam and Eve were in perfect paradise, and the devil introduced them to the temptations of sin and all the attendant consequences of sorrow, pain and constant agonies followed. In the words of God, Satan is always seeking to destroy us, and God's advice to us to be self-controlled and alert. Your enemy the devil prowls around us like a roaring lion looking for something to devour. The devil does everything in his power to blind people to the truth. He seeks our allegiance and worship. He has filled the world with lies to keep us in darkness. The evil force in the world is real and powerful. People suffer from his influence. He and his tribes enslave and imprison countless people. In the Holy Quran God says, "For Satan is to man an avowed enemy." Since Satan and his host of demons are such powerful beings, how can man stand up to them? That is the predicament of the human being.

According to the holy books, the Quran and the Bible, those demons have existed since Adam and Eve. And from when they ate the fruit of knowledge to this day, we are influenced by evil forces. We are in constant battle as these forces rage without mercy against us. They are invisible to our physical dimension, and their invisible world remains mysterious and enigmatic to us. The Gallup poll in 2001 found that more than 40% of Americans believed that people on earth could sometimes be possessed by evil forces, and the percentages are much higher in the Indian and Arab cultures.

In the Final Analysis...

The Seven Deadly Enemies are operating independently, and we have little or no control over them.

Thus, we struggle all our lives to undo the damage done by these enemies.

We are helpless in the face of their attacks.

The old wisdom indicates: our existence is merely a cruel joke.

<u>**Steps to protect one self from the seven deadly enemies**</u>

The first enemy: our wicked nature. We all are under the mercy of our Almighty God; we cannot do anything about this enemy. God has initially programmed us since conception with the wicked force first. We are limited in our understanding of God's wisdom in that. Therefore, we may need to seek salvation through His mercy and compassion. We have to be mindful of our dark soul; it may push us to commit heinous crimes toward ourselves and others.

The second enemy: sly mind.

1. Watch your mind carefully when you have inner monologues; do not let ideas swim in your head.
2. Do not believe what your mind may tell you. It may give you an inaccurate perception about the world around you, because the mind's job is to exaggerate fears.
3. Try to challenge your mind to see the bright side of life.
4. Face every day with fresh spirit and do not hold onto the past; it is a dead leaf.

5. Cultivate your inner garden; it is inevitable there will be weeds growing inside of you

6. Try to live life and do not make an attempt to understand it.

7. See the beauty in things and do not let your mind show you the broken glasses.

8. Learn movement meditation, in which you focus on what you do right then and there.

9. Have a leash for your mind and do not let it run you like a wild horse.

10. Do not sweat the small stuff; let it go. Life is a very short journey.

11. Try to control your mind, and do not let your mind control you

The third enemy: illness.

1. Exercise daily.

2. Eat 70% of your daily food as natural and non-cooked.

3. Avoid eating dead animals.

4. As soon as you find out that you have an autoimmune disease, you need to seek non-traditional medicine also; give yourself a broad means of treatments.

5. Have courage and the mindset that you will defeat the illness.

6. Wash your hands many times throughout the day.

7. Avoid contaminated food.

8. Take supplements to ward off attack by viruses and bacteria.

9. Organize your sleeping cycle.

10. Go into a fasting program, and rely on vegetable juices during fasts.

11. Never allow yourself to be constipated; you should have an enema every few weeks. Or regulate your bowel movement at least twice daily.

12. Try to be mindful of the childhood desire to be sick; it can be unconscious.

13. Illness is a conspiracy the unconscious mind may cook it and then manifest in your body. Thus, be aware of the wish to be sick.

The fourth enemy: aging.

1. Exercise daily.
2. Organize your circadian rhythm.
3. Eat a diet of mostly vegetables and fruits.
4. Eat a lot of fish.
5. Have inner serenity; do not let worry control your life.
6. Laugh a lot and have a positive attitude.
7. Do not be too serious about life; no one gets out of it alive!
8. Avoid serious exposure to the sun.
9. Loving supportive partner can slow the aging process
10. Involve in learning musical instrument, it will create new synapses in your brain.

The fifth enemy: people.

1. You cannot control people's behavior, but you can control your reaction to their behavior.
2. Try to be kind to people.
3. Do not waste your time with the dysfunctions of people.
4. Be mindful when you deal with people, and teach them to respect you.
5. Be more listener than talker.
6. Be around positive, uplifting people.
7. Do not try to please people; try to please yourself first.
8. Be assertive in what you like and dislike in your life.
9. You also need to understand that no matter what you do, there are some people who are envious, jealous, aggressive, and who will occasionally violate you. Just try to protect yourself from them.
10. Finally, be independent of good and bad judgment of others.
11. Never, never defend yourself for any accusation.

The sixth enemy: mishaps.

1. You cannot do anything about mishaps; just be careful in what you do.
2. Try to send positive vibrations to the world.
3. Be mindful of the Karmic law in the universe. Always do the good, because doing well or bad is not for other people, it is all for you. As the old wisdom says, "you reap what you sow."

The seventh enemy: evil forces.

1. Have strong faith in God and always seek His salvation.
2. Practice daily prayers and meditation.
3. Be around good-natured people.
4. Clean your heart of any malice, and let compassion reside within, let compassion guide your through this life.
5. Have good intentions in what you do in your life.
6. Try to be giving person as much as you can, that can ward of the evil force from your lives
7. Divot portion of your time for spiritual practices.
8. Guard yourself from this force by have noble intentions.

Chapter Six

Talib's Paradigm of Self Alienation

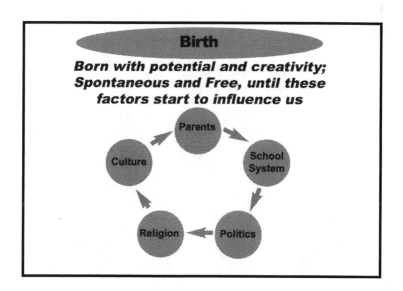

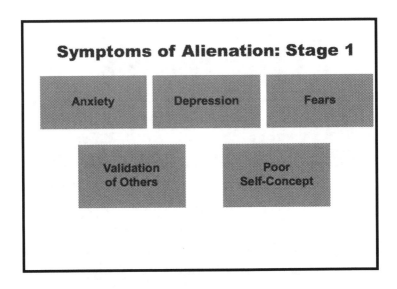

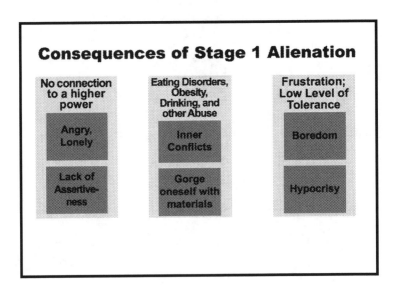

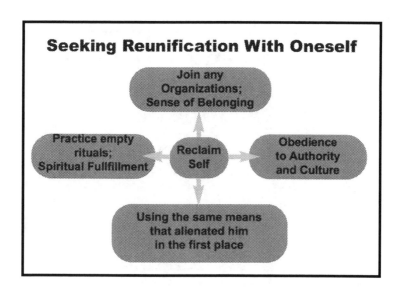

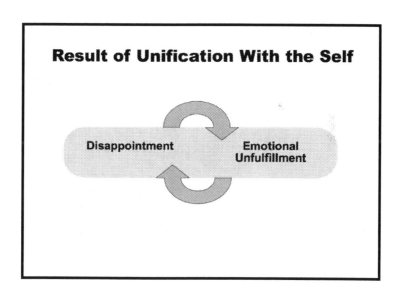

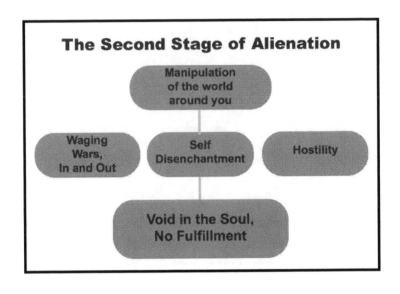

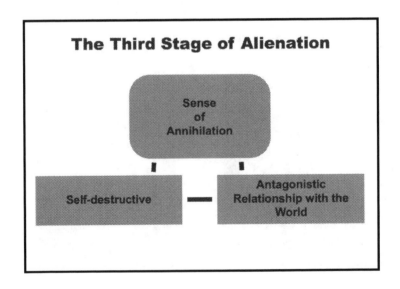

Fourth & Final Stage of Alienation

This is the current state of the human condition, unless we redeem ourselves to be connected to the main source of love.

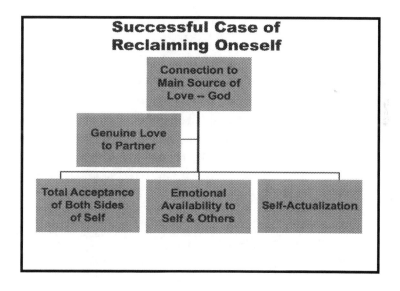

Successful Case of Reclaiming Oneself

The Alienation of Mankind

As we have moved forward in our civilization, man has become alien to himself. So, suffering is inevitable. Self –realization is in the distant past. The world is the object of man's creation, but collectively his desires and greed have turned against him. Consequently they became barriers to allowing him to be in touch with his true essence and humanity.

Marx had the best definition of alienation: a variety of human states, including powerlessness, apathy, loneliness, and a reduction of self-worth. Some fall into disassociation, in which the individual separates from society, and contradicts some social norms and conditions.

Finn and Donald, in their essay "On Losing the Soul", an essay on the social psychology of religion, (1995, State University of New York, Albany, NY) defined alienation as guilt that has a social origin. This guilt is generated by social roles a person has to play, feeling he has no control over some major aspect of his life. It is a sense of degradation, produced by being forced to participate in the social necessities that one hates.

Throughout history man participated greatly to enslave himself. For example, he created idols to worship, metaphorically speaking. By doing that, he transformed his self into things, attributing great power to this idol, giving a life to it. Soon, he started to experience himself through his creations. He is in touch with himself only through worshiping idols. He becomes estranged from his own life's forces, and from the wealth of his own potential. He was only in touch with himself indirectly, through submission to idols. The more man transformed his own power to the idol, the more he became dead and empty.

What are the idols? They can be a state, a nationality, wealth, a person, possessions, position, statues, a religion, and so on. Thus, he can experience alienation in many forms in his life. Once he assigns a power to those objects, they assume lives of their own.

In modern times, man has replaced the idol with the cult of personality. Pathological dictators have taken advantage of man's vulnerability, trying to suck him dry, and inflicted enormous pain and suffering on him. Presently, that is what we are witnessing in the cruelty of despots who rule most of the Middle East.

Marx, Freud and Erich Fromm articulated that modern society blocks the possibility of human coherence, while Sartre indicated that an individual is not a whole; he is fragmented. There is alienation and self-integration, which is self-alienation that takes the falsified personality of oneself for a true personality. Man labors day and night to fulfill the urge of this false imposed personality. Evidently, this is the source of our pain and anguish.

Psychological alienation is when people live in an atmosphere of artificially fabricated external values, like money or position. People tend to see themselves through those objects which they have created. Man has separated his existence from his essence. Thus, he is anxious, and depressed.

He relinquished his true essence to outside objects. At home he feels emasculated because of the overwhelming demands of his family. His family's life is no longer providing him with satisfaction. According to psychological research, **he feels like a blind horse, running fast without knowing the direction**. The demands of his family and children are endless and he has to fulfill his family obligations, but in return he feels that he is fading. There is no emotional fulfillment or affection inside his home. Thus, the divorce rate skyrockets. Home is no longer a safe place, and child abuse is rampant. Consequently, alienation is the norm today for a majority of people.

The many faces of alienation. There is alienation from people around us, because we have to give in to, or abide by, social customs, or the manners and traditions of society. If the individual does not submit to such roles, he will be ostracized. A person wants to be in touch with himself through the validation of others, and if he does not receive such validation he may become hostile and project his aggression onto people around him. Even if he receives such validation or approval, he knows in the bottom of his soul it is not true, just superficial, and does not touch his core being.

These are the faces of alienation:

1. Alienation from nature around us. We live like exiles in nature, with no harmony. We have abused nature to the maximum; with toxicity and pollution in every part of our nature: in the forests, the rivers, the land, and the air. Needless to say, the effect of carbon monoxide on our environment has manifested as global warming. There is a certain detachment from nature, and that can have a profound impact on us psychologically, as we feel alien to nature. We do not respect our environment, and the environment is angry with us. This is why today we see many changes and serious attacks from nature like floods, earthquakes, or environmental change and global warming.

2. Alienation from God is isolation from the higher self, in which we are essentially living in a constant state of dying, or a state of separation from life's forces, as Buddha proclaimed. Man dehumanized himself through his creation, God sent several messengers to free man from the bondage of his ego, and in return he created layers and layers of shackles to chain himself more and more. Thus, he started to worship religion itself, not the creator of religions -- God. Man focused on the insignificant details of religion, and he uses religion as a tool to separate him from his follow humans. Eventually religion becomes the source of his pain and cruelty, rather than the agent of soothing and meaning. He is governed by his perceptions of religion, not by the actual messages of God. In other words, man is governed by the product of his own brain, not by the essence of God's message. Therefore, the greatest cause of human alienation has been religion, because each religion considered the beliefs of other religions as anathema, deprived of the mercy of God.

3. Alienation from the body. Man starts to abuse his body and develop all sorts of illness, and becomes a helpless creature

whose body becomes a burden on him. This is why we see epidemics of obesity and diabetes. Sadly enough, the body becomes the battleground for most of his psychological or internal conflicts. Even sexual fulfillment, which many consider the most enjoyable pleasure, becomes mechanical and is performed as just mere duty. Another wonderful bodily pleasure is defecating, but he is no longer able to enjoy it, because he has developed a chronic case of constipation. When a person loses control over their outside world, they want to exercise some control over their feces. Chronic constipation is so common today, and that can deprive a person of the joy of daily life. Carrying poisons or waste of your food inside of you for a couple of days or even a single day, can have serious health ramifications for your body.

4. Alienation from the concept of gain. Man works so hard to accumulate wealth, he becomes a slave to it; the object of his wealth becomes his master. Man has lost his integrity and pride for the sake of money. Man's insatiable desire to have more money makes him greedy, with a sense of being helpless in the face of money. The most alienating element to man is money, because money has an overruling power against the individual and his place in society, or it can be a measurement of human value.

    For the sake of money, man compromised his integrity, intelligence and goodness. Often, money transforms fidelity into infidelity, love into hate, hate into love, virtue into vice, vice into virtue, servant into master, master into servant, idiocy into intelligence, and intelligence into idiocy (Marx, 1844). Money has enslaved most human beings. Man finds himself free only in activities like eating, dressing, procreating and dwelling. Therefore, he no longer feels himself to be anything but an animal, because he has an estranged spiritual life and has become a slave of commodities. **Modern man's life is like a kitchen full**

of condiments, but with no food. This is true alienation to all human beings.

To illustrate the above example; condiments but no food analogy, we have more communication systems, but we have less real contact with each other. We have more food, but we are getting sicker. We have more entertainment, but we are more depressed. We have more laws to organize our lives, but we have more child and spousal abuse. We talk a lot about love, but we have the highest divorce rate in human history. We talk a lot about peace, but we produce more sophisticated, lethal arms to fight each other. As Soren Kierkegaard, the existential philosopher said "that is the clear indication of human absurdity".

5. Alienation in the work place. A man holds a position and he starts to abuse the people around him through that position; he inflicts a lot of pain on them. Why? He wants to assuage his alienation from his self and to alleviate his internal conflicts. Of course, all that is superficial and never cuts deep to the roots of the problem, because he is not addressing the real causes of his pain: the separation from self, and the separation from the higher power. As far as work is concerned, he is becoming tyrannical. Thus, man feels homeless at work; there is no sense of belonging, and he feels exhausted physically and drained mentally. At work he suffers passively and his restless soul is no longer part of his surroundings. That is why we see a high degree of burn out in the workplace, and a lot of stress.

The Dynamic of Alienation. Man in alienated society feels he is not an end in himself; he is a means used by the establishment. Thus, he becomes alien even to his own spirit. He becomes an object for something else, such as religion, politicians, wealth, or position. Carol Rogers came up with a wonderful concept. There is an ideal self, and there is an actual self; there must be congruence between those concepts within us. But we gradually become a stranger to ourselves. Our real feelings and experiences become twisted, distorted and stretched into a mold of the appropriate self that meets society's expectations.

Mankind's self-alienation has reached such a degree that it can experiment its own destruction. This is why the alienated man becomes abusive to his fellow man and to his female companion. The male runs the show in most spheres of our lives. In return, he takes revenge on the female, subjecting her to all manner of abuse, due to his unconscious fear of castration. But he is castrated by the establishment, whether it is a religion, a political system, or even the tyrannical rules of society. The question remains in the soul of man: how can he be a virtuous and compassionate member of human society, if most of his surrounding environment wants to mold him to be part of the herd? Often, man does not want to face this reality, and tries to numb himself through substance use, or through sex, or through accumulation of wealth, or through having some control over his fellow humans.

We have specific needs to be fulfilled; our bodily need for food, social needs for the expression of love and to be loved, and for a sense of belonging. However, sometimes the sense of belonging may alienate us as well, because it may transform us to see our own world through the lenses of society, which often perpetuates approval seeking from others. That is the ultimate alienation.

The Alienated Self. If we do not respect ourselves, we are peculiarly enthralled by everyone we see. Since our self-image is not attainable, we create a false notion of us. We flatter ourselves by thinking this compulsion to please others is an attractive trait. Hence, the phenomenon called alienation from self is in its advanced stages. We no longer answer the phone, because someone might want something from us and we cannot say no, without self-reproachment (Joan Didion, *Slouching Toward Bethlehem*).

Hence, although our soul is infinite, and connects with all cosmic powers, once we alienate this soul it becomes like a dog that runs after any bone thrown to him. Horney indicated the self is not to be found through searching, but something to be realized through struggle. This struggle is best expressed in terms of an awakening, or becoming conscious of one's role in life. She also reported that alienation is the feeling of not being an active determining force in one's own life. Man has lost his autonomy and self-regulation in being an authentic and active agent in one's life. In the interaction between the individual and the world he lives in, he may see himself as powerful, or as a self-effacing person. He excessively depends on the approval, ideas, guidance, feelings, and opinions of others, and clearly feels the world or others to be a more potent factor in his life. He has little or no feeling that he is an active agent in his own life.

The ugly face of alienation. War is part of the alienated self; the emptiness and meaninglessness of modern life, the terrible loneliness of the individual, his isolation and drifting, and his attempts to not see reality. In alienation, there are characteristics of modern civilization which did not exist in previous ages. Man is unhappy because his consciousness is divided against itself. Separated from its essence, he seeks inner fulfillment through artificial means, created throughout human history.

Modern people are losing the ability to either rejoice or grieve with their whole heart. Modern man is unable to cry or laugh in the depth of his being. The alienated person despises society, and vents his hatred on the barren wasteland of materialism. Society becomes a living death to him. The alienated person lives in the world of mediocrity, enwrapped in his own solitude and loneliness.

Plato and Aristotle have a classical statement: man's distinctive happiness, and man's distinctive flourishing will only be realized when he realizes himself.

Rousseau's claim: find a form of association which will defend the person and the goods of each member, with the collective force of all. Each individual can unite himself with others, but obeys no one but himself. R.D. Lang indicated that alienation as our present destiny is achieved only by outrageous violence, perpetrated by human beings on other human beings.

Self-realization. Man has the desire and tendency to engage in many activities which promote mutual human survival and psychological well-being, by means of emotional connections with other people and society. The goal is to be like a child completely caught up in the moment, not burdened by the ideas about self that have been handed down by cultures, because culture may deform the individual.

Internalizing alienation. Individuals are no different in their need to control perceived sources of anxiety and threat so they can maintain mental and psychological balance. Attempts to emulate the source of danger take a more socialized and political form of expression. The basic process of self-alienation remains the same: internalizing threats, or becoming one with it through emulation. That will bridge quickly and thoroughly bridge the wide gap between the inferior's feeling of worthlessness, weakness, and guilt, and the imagined omnipotence of the perceived aggressor. At the core of the process lies a relationship of inferiority between the fearsome and the fearful, between the powerful and the powerless, the wealthy and the impoverished, the conqueror and the conquered.

In a sad example, the feeling of the Arab toward himself has been inculcated with inferiority over many decades. Because Arabs lived under oppression for centuries, their sense of alienation is imbedded in their conscious mind. This is why the amount of aggression and cruelty they inflict on each other is beyond imagination.

The emotional dynamic of alienation. Alienation = Fear + hate + guilt + self-pity. A person, who does not value himself, generates guilt in a mode of self-hate which leads to personal guilt. The system does not value the person, and generates social guilt or alienation. Personal guilt amplified leads to depersonalization, which can lead to separation from his own body. Impersonal, or social, guilt, amplified, leads to, impersonalization. The feeling of alienation always slows down the rate of recovery from depression and anxiety, and other mental imbalance.

The characteristics of alienation include powerlessness, mindlessness, isolation, loss of autonomy, and self-estrangement. Powerlessness is the probability that an individual's own behavior cannot determine the outcomes, or reinforcement, that he seeks. Society adversely influences an individual's development making him abnormal, narrow, egoist, and selfish; in other words, it makes him a person who suffers from serious pathologies.

Nietzsche indicated the core of human essence is passion, but all ordered society puts passion to sleep. For the individual to regain his healthy passion, he has to break the chain with which society binds him. Nietzsche surmised that modern man finds himself annihilated, and lives with constructed values. He questioned why society is fascinated with scientific truth, and universal moral principles, because science has objectified humans and distanced them from nature, each other and themselves. The universal moral principles that have formed human existence are according to ideologies disconnected from the way people actually experience life, and caused people to see life as a chore.

The three characteristic states for all living things including humans:

1. The state of being.
2. The state of harmony.
3. The state of awareness.

A bird enjoys being bird, a tree enjoys being a tree, but man is self –conscious, and he is not going to enjoy himself. The first and second states are for animals and plants, while the third is for humans. Once he develops an awareness of himself, then man has to face his mortality, and that makes him more anxious.

The non-alienated human being. An individual who experiences the richness of his own individuality is non-alienated. He experiences his own power, and trusts in himself, because he is unique, and feels that he will leave a lasting impression on the sands of life. He sees the supreme aim of life, which allows him to reach his full potential. He sees that God bestowed on him unimaginable power, and he is able to relinquish and free himself from compulsion and anxiety. He is connected to the main sources of life; he relates to himself and is in touch with his core being. Therefore, he can relate to others in a healthy fashion. All of this happens without overestimating himself, but rather by utilizing the infinite richness of his self. Such development of man can lead to the unfolding of his whole humanity, and emancipate him from his greed. Once he reaches this level of awareness, he becomes the agent of his own change, and relates to himself without going through others to connect with himself.

A Summary of the mechanism of alienation

We come to this world as free individuals, and we strive to be happy and independent. But unfortunately, we are faced with numerous cultural systems (parents, society, school systems, political systems, and religion) all of which influence us profoundly and unconsciously. Gradually, the individual starts to be stripped of his own essence, or his own true self. He becomes alien to himself; because he feels he is not living to meet his expected self or his full potential. The process starts from childhood. And once the individual becomes alien to himself, he may well suffer from loneliness, anxiety, depression and becomes a fearful creature, as well as looking scary and acting impulsively. The individual cannot stand to be that way, faces apprehension that he has to do something about where he stands in life. He wants to reclaim himself from the sense of alienation he developed as a result of living in this world. He looks for the kernel of truth to actualize his essence that, *he wants to love and be loved*. Or, he may yearn to be reunited with the alien part of himself, or to have a union with another loved object.

What might he do to reclaim himself from the sense of alienation? Sadly, he must resort to the same factors that alienated him in the first place. In such a case he may use religion, the approval of others, or joining an organization to feel the sense of belonging. But sooner or later, he has to discover that the broken car which brought him to this place is unable to take him back. Or the salt he uses to season his food is spoiled in itself, metaphorically speaking. In other words, the virus that made him sick is not going to cure him. But his foolish mind does understand that, but he is desperate to escape his alienation.

At this stage of his alienated life, he becomes disenchanted with the whole process of living, which does not bring any meaning or fulfillment to his life. Unfortunately, he then turns to different methods to free himself from the alienated self, and these are destructive methods. He may start to abuse his body through overeating, abusing substances, smoking, or being a hypocrite in dealing with society. Or, he resorts to the empty rituals of his religion, thus losing the true connection with the primary force in the universe. He gorges himself with the material consumption. He may develop some mental or psychological difficulties. For example, he may become anxious, fearful, phobic, develop OCD, get burned out at work, or in his marriage. He has no sexual satisfactions, is unfulfilled in his marriage, and is bored with life in general. In other words, life to him may become a painful chore, not a journey of joy.

From there, he may move to a higher stage of alienation, in which he becomes aggressive and angry at the world around him on a large scale. He becomes hostile toward others. He may not hesitate to attack or wage a war on his fellow humans. He invents all manner of defense mechanisms to justify the destructive means of his alienated self. He becomes numb, pathetic, and indifferent to the people around him, and to himself. Physically, he may develop a variety of diseases, such as obesity or diabetes. These are metabolic diseases which result from lack of discipline over his desire to eat. The alienated man becomes careless when it comes to his own temple of the soul, his body.

Spiritually, he becomes bankrupt, and uses religion to manipulate his surroundings and his relationship with others. He loses the connection to the higher power. He may become superficial, and take advantage of others. He may develop insatiable desires to have more and more, and there is no limit to his unbridled greed and selfishness. As a result, he becomes an empty being, and suffers silently.

This is the process by which the individual reclaims himself, and lives meaningfully:

1. Provide the individual with unconditional positive regard.
2. Provide the individual with nurturing and supportive surroundings.
3. Provide the individual with a hobby which he may practice daily.
4. He must focus on his personal, signature strengths.
5. Consume a very healthy diet and thereby avoid constipation.
6. Follow a stricter schedule for sleep and awakening.
7. Engage in a very meaningful, loving relationship.
8. Be independent of the good and bad judgment of others.
9. Allow the individual to actualize his potential.
10. Undo the old scripts, and create a new script that makes him feel he is a worthwhile individual.

Chapter Seven

The Domination of Humans by Irrationality

The landscape of irrationality. Rationality is not a strong trait in human behavior; the majority of human traits are manifested irrationally. If you observe daily human behavior, which can easily be seen. Our greatest irrationality seems often to be associated with short-sighted thinking, which dominates most of us. Irrational thoughts often occur in the minds of all people. Intelligence does not make someone immune to irrational thoughts. These thoughts typically clutter the mind with feelings of resentment, anger, and distaste. Hence, thoughts are based on internal defense mechanisms that we develop to mitigate personal anger, or in an attempt to avoid facing the truth about ourselves or our immediate circumstances.

We define irrationality as thoughts, emotions, and behaviors that lead to self-defeating consequences, or which significantly interferes with the survival and happiness of the organism. Thus, literally thousands of major irrationalities existed in all societies, and in virtually all people. Irrationality persists despite people's conscious determination to change these disturbing thoughts. But, these thoughts are ingrained in the layers of our unconscious mind, and they appear to us when the situation arises.

The human dilemma. Albert Ellis indicated that humans often engage in irrational behavior, we fight, we start wars, we kill, and we are self-destructive. We are petty and vindictive; we act out when we do not get our way. We abuse our spouses, neglect our children, rationalize projection and stereotypes, and we contradict and deceive ourselves in countless ways. We act inconsistently, ignore relevance, jump to conclusion and say or believe things that do not make good sense. Obviously, the ultimate motivating force behind human irrationality is egocentrism, which is the natural human tendency to view everything in relationship to oneself; to be self-centered. Daniel Kahneman indicated that people are not fully rational and they make very bad choices. If they reflect upon them, they would do differently. People tend to frame things very narrowly; their perspective of what takes place is often distorted by their interpretations.

Does the human brain have a tendency to be irrational? The answer is yes, and psychological researches has demonstrated, time and time again, the mind's tendency to follow the path of irrational thinking, simply if the brain is subjected to outside influences. For example; anger, fear, stress, anxiety and depression are toxic to the brain. Studies show that when these appear, they will shut down the **prefrontal cortex**, the part of the brain responsible for decision making, correcting errors, and assessing situations. That is why you see people go crazy or act irrationally when they are faced with rage, frustration, or disappointment, because the rational part of the brain is shut down.

Socrates said, a person could train his mind the way gymnasts train their muscles. We train our minds to produce irrational thinking. We live in a culture that often encourages irrationality and suspends logic.

Confirmation biases are the tendency to search for or interpret information in a way that confirms one's perception, leading to statistical errors. It is a type of cognitive bias and represents an error of inductive inference toward confirmation of the hypothesis. These phenomena actively seek out and assign more weight to evidence which confirms the hypothesis, and ignore or give less weight to evidence that could disprove the hypothesis. As such, it is a form of selection bias in collecting evidence, and such bias belongs to the territory of irrationality.

On the other hand, when we are faced with a situation or person, we tend to draw all the old materials from our unconscious mind to support our judgment, or our position toward the person or the situation. Consequently, irrationality plays a major role in such judgment. Our unconscious mind tends to bring forward unwanted materials, after they have been passed through the conscious to the unconscious mind. Definitely, our unconscious mind tends to exaggerate events and capitalize on the negative part of our experiences, and on the irrational side of our experiences.

Society and irrationality. Humans primarily are not creatures of reason, but of habits. We have the potential to be rational and logical, but that is not what we are. As Philip Zimbardo put it: "I have been primarily interested in how and why ordinary people do unusual things, things that seem alien to their nature." Why do good people sometimes act in evil ways? Why do smart people sometimes do dumb or irrational things? Sharon Begley, in her book *The Limits of Reason*, indicated that humans are bad at reasoning. Psychologists have been documenting this since 1960, while philosophers have been discussing the failure of reason since the dawn of time.

Humans are very good at persuading each other to believe in very stupid things, yet very bad at recognizing what was, in fact, very stupid. Henry Morris said rational thinkers have not always been the most insightful and open-minded people. Throughout history, thinking rationally has often become a guise for repressive attitudes toward the new or unconventional. David Ropeik indicated the brain is only the organ with which we <u>think</u> we think. Its job is not to win a Nobel Prize, or to pass a math test. Its job is to get us to tomorrow. It is a survival mechanism, and it plays many tricks to get us to tomorrow. It is not as adept when we need it to rationalize and reason, let alone make us happy. It is a sly brain, or the sly mind!

Freud knew that the conscious motives for our behavior were not the real causes of our behavior. There are numerous unconscious reasons for our behavior. The prime motives are sexual and aggressive in origin. Both motives are basically irrational. However, our behavior makes sense from the motive itself, even if they are very destructive motives. Douglas Kendrick indicated in his book, that human decisions are eminently rational, or hopelessly irrational. Our choices are highly rational and amazingly self-serving. However, social psychologists have uncovered countless ways in which people's decisions are short-sighted, ill-informed and otherwise shockingly biased. It is the decoy effect, or the gambler's fallacy, which makes human decisions that are relentlessly and hopelessly irrational. We are born to be biased, irrational beings in many aspects of our lives.

For example, look at marriage, a cultural institution which has much irrationality in its application. A couple becomes slaves for each other. However, from an evolutionary perspective, we want to ensure our survival as a species, through offspring. Such irrationality came from Adam and Eve, whose irrationality brought suffering to mankind.

The irrationality of fear. A little fear can be very motivational for us, but also can be very irrational, because fear can give you a false perception of reality. Exaggerated fears are part of anxiety, and often, modern man has been infected with irrational fears which have no basis in reality. It is in man's mind and disturbs him consistently, taking the joy out of life. On a conscious level, man knows his fear is irrational, but somehow he has lost the ability to control his rational mind in this particular area. In irrational thinking, normally the mind takes over the personality, while in rational thinking man takes control over the mind. Sadly enough, that is rare; irrational or undefined fears have a strong grip on us. For example, anxiety or panic attacks are basically irrational fears, or false perceptions of our reality. People fight to rid themselves of such disturbing thoughts, which keep occurring, even without obvious causes.

Albert Ellis, a pioneer in the field of psychology, addressed the irrationality of human beings. He wrote numerous books and gave thousands of lectures about how much irrational thinking damaged our psychological well-being, and brought misery to our lives. His approach was to identify irrational thinking, and then learn to replace it with rational thinking. Most people do not know how to do this, so that is the role of the therapist, who has the skills to identify irrational thinking and help patients replace it, according to RET (Rational Emotive Therapy), of which Ellis was the founder.

Fears arise within us when we put demands on ourselves to perform perfectly. The fear of irrationality may arise when we fear people and their opinions of us. Fear of irrationality can take place unconsciously within our psyche. When we have catastrophic thinking, it tends to deplete us of our energy, and negatively color our perspectives on life. Catastrophic thinking is very irrational thinking, but somehow it prevails among the majority of people. Thus, the rate of depression and anxiety is on the rise worldwide. Perhaps our brain is not designed to cope with modern man's incredible technological advancements. Our brain is designed for hunting and gathering, not for air conditioning and with no animals to attack us. Modern man is suffering from overwhelming anxiety, and most of it is from irrational, or baseless, fears.

The dynamic of irrationality. Irrational thinking is something that plagues us all from time to time, and can cause a lot of problems. Irrational thoughts tend to come from our negative emotions rather than from logic. Often, we are not congruent with the world around us, and that can prevent us from going about our daily lives, because the core of the problem is that such thoughts are self-perpetuating and confirming. Sadly, **we can develop an addiction to our irrational thoughts**, and our lives can become living hells. Once you allow irrational thoughts to go through your mind, they will become stronger, and will attack you without mercy. You need to challenge your irrational thoughts with your personal experiences in order to defeat them. We have tremendous irrational fears, often based on false perceptions of reality. This fear is managing our lives, taking away all our happiness and inner peace. Another widespread belief in human irrationality which is we believe irrational things about ourselves, rather than believing what the evidence tells us.

The philosophy of irrationality. Existentialism sees our existence fundamentally irrational in nature, and focuses on the subjective irrational character of human existence. Sartre postulated that the absurdity of human existence is the necessary result of our attempt to live a life of meaning and purpose in an indifferent, uncertain, and uncaring universe. There is no perfect and absolute vantage point from which human action or choice can be said to be rational. In the same vein, Kierkegaard indicated that humans are caught in a web of subjectivity, from which they cannot escape. In the end we must all make choices which are not based upon fixed, rational standards, choices which are just as likely to be wrong as right. Kierkegaard called this a leap of faith. It is an irrational choice, but ultimately a necessary one, if a person wants to lead a full, authentic human existence. The absurdity of our lives is never actually overcome, but it is embraced in the hope that by making the best choices, we will finally achieve a union with the infinite, absolute power of God.

Albert Camus' perspective about the pseudo-solution to the absurd nature of reality is that human reasoning fits so poorly with reality as we find it. Organisms, including humans, are often assumed to be hard-wired by evolution to try to make optimal decisions, to the best of their knowledge. As David Brooks clearly indicated in his book, we have to learn to love the irrational mind. We all make dehumanizing decisions, because there is a serious flaw in human nature; perhaps we are amputated from human nature. Humans are deeply interdependent creatures, who learn, and even forget, our personalities from the people with whom we surround ourselves.

Steven Pinker said that our lives are not governed by passion, instincts or IQ, because our irrationality stretches the dimensions of instinct and feeling, and it rails against reason. The main tide of irrationality is the emergence of literary romanticism, itself a form of irrationalism. Frederick the Great said every man has a wild beast within him. Plato had a different perspective about man. He sees man as a rational being. Oscar Wilde also sees man as a rational animal, which always loses his temper when he is called upon to act in accordance with the dictates of reason. Wilde also said we have reason, but at the same time, we have irrational appetites, which we call desires. Nevertheless, Aristotle indicated that humans have a purpose, and have the ability to reason -- characteristics that set humans apart from all other creatures in nature.

Freud proposed that the unconscious mind manages our lives, by the forces of irrationality. He also viewed mental processes to be energy flow within us, while behavior is motivated by sex and aggression. The expression of these motives can be in direct conflict with societies and civilization. Then the price of civilization is misery, which forfeits our happiness and induces a sense of guilt. He also said, man is not gentle, friendly, or a loving creature, but possesses powerful desires for aggression.

Clearly, most research has shown that human beings, yourself included, move ultimately by self-interest and desire. Our actions, even those that seem to arise out of love for another, are ultimately motivated by the desire for self-gratification, because self-interest is an inseparable part of being human. The challenging question remains: are we at least sometimes unselfish? Many social psychologists conclude that human beings behave irrationally. Max Bazerman, in his book, *Judgment in Managerial Decision Making,* cited numerous studies showing that humans rely on irrational beliefs and rules of thumb when they make decisions. Frederick Nietzsche said man is absolutely not the crown of creation; every creature stands beside him at the same stage of perfection.

There are certain common irrational beliefs which infect most of us. For example:

1. Mistakes are never acceptable. If I make one, 1 am incompetent.

2. When somebody disagrees with me, it is a personal attack against me.
3. To be content in life, 1 must be liked by all people, and succeed in everything.
4. My true value as an individual depends on what others think of me.
5. If 1 am not involved in an intimate relationship, 1 am completely alone.
6. There is no gray area; success is white, failure is black.
7. Nothing ever turns out the way you want it to.
8. If the outcome was not perfect, it was a complete failure.
9. I am in absolute control of my life. If something bad happens, it is my fault.
10. The past always repeats itself. If it was true then, it must be true now.

Conclusion. Twisted thinking is a psychological disorder, and irrational belief is the source of our disturbance. Our life will be more productive if we avoid the negative frame of mind brought on by irrationality. However, irrational thinking dominates human thinking, whether we like it or not, because society, throughout human history often thinks irrationally. It has some benefits occasionally, but mostly it can bring agony. Basically, we are born with the tendency toward irrational thinking, which may lead to irrational behavior. Certain assumptions we have about our life can be counterproductive to our well-being, or to our survival as a species. Bear in mind, when you do things over and over and society accepts them, it does not mean those things are correct. The conclusion to be made is, human culture has abundant irrationality, and we consider that quite normal. It has almost become the fabric of society. But overall, irrationality can be the seed of our disturbance, and may cause enormous pain and suffering. Or, it may deplete our resources, such as military spending, which is based on our irrational fear of each others.

Chapter Eight

How the Individual Can Be Deformed by Cultural Practices

When we talk about culture, we talk about metabolizing the daily experiences of culture, and it becomes part and parcel of our body and psyche.

How we define culture. Culture refers to the cumulative deposit of knowledge, experiences, values, attitudes, meaning, hierarchies, religion, notions of time, roles, spatial relations, the concept of the universe, and myths. The essential core of culture consists of traditional ideas and especially their attached values. It is the sum of learned behavior. It is a collective programming of the mind that distinguishes the members of one group, or category of people, from another. Culture is the core of living, and cultivates individuals to be subordinate to society. It is the heritage of our ancestors.

Cultural ethnocentrism is the belief that one's own culture is superior to that of others. It is a form of reductionism that reduces others to non-beings, in a culture that can produce toxic ideas of a superior race. This concept has psychological roots. We often have feelings of venerability, or exaggerated ego. Such notions are developed out of our weakness. Thus, we have an assumption that we are better than other people, or our history is better than your history, or my people are better than your people. All of these concepts are part of human stupidity. We like to put ourselves above others, to make us feel better. But in reality, we do not feel better, it is just a pseudo-feeling.

The idea that a certain race is better than another is ingrained in the unconscious of the majority of people. They may find some relief from the burden of their ego, which keeps nagging them to be different. Our ego is like a spoiled child; it needs satisfaction to keep our inner conflicts at a bay. Rarely, you find people who think of themselves as equal with everybody else. Such thinking requires a great deal of psychological maturity, which the majority of us are lacking. We spend enormous energy in finding our differences rather than finding our similarities. However, we are idiots; we really do not know what is good for ourselves. We are involved in a constant struggle that is non-productive for anyone. It is better to look at our journey on earth as a short one, and we all are the children of God. As Gibran put, "we all are fingers from one loving hand of God."

However, there are no superior or inferior races. We each have certain circumstances that provide people with opportunities to excel, or with opportunities for failure. For example, American culture promotes success, while Arab culture promotes failure. It all depends on cultural factors that either bring the best or worst out of the individual. Normally, a free society tends to promote the good of the individual, while an oppressive culture suppresses human creativity. This mechanism has operated within every culture since the beginning of time.

What caused us to have a free or an oppressive culture in the first place? Certain historical events took place, which shaped the perspectives of the people, in either culture. Based upon such perspective, society produced these two basic types of people. However, the free, or civilized, culture looks down on the oppressive culture, and accuses their people of being less intelligent, and backward. That can be a very harsh judgment and we need to be mindful that such a culture has been living in hardship. Sadly those cultures are controlled by people who do not have the good of others in their heart, or by idiots, the rulers, who are abusive to the people.

If humans are left to their will, they would not hesitate to abuse each others; it is a part of human psychology. We love to have control over others, and if the situation permits, we would not hesitate an inch to abuse or dominate others. This is part of the "garbage" portion of the human psychological makeup; there is no escape from it. The Western world has realized this, and designed laws to control and organize societal behavior, rather than leave it to the whim of the people. Unfortunately, Eastern culture has left it to people's conscience, or to religion. We all know very well that religious teaching has not made a dent in human behavior, because people focus on the ritual part of religion, and not on faith. Faith is what can truly purify the human soul from the garbage of culture.

Culture and the unconscious mind. Culture is like mass hypnosis. Most of the materials that we have in any culture are absorbed unconsciously. We observe the traditions, the customs, the habits, the practices, or any cultural ideas consciously. And since the conscious mind is unable to store them for a long period, we store them in the unconscious mind, and they appear whenever circumstances call them. For example, if you grow up in a culture that thinks all Arabs are terrorists, as soon as you see a profile that fits the description in your unconscious mind, you behave according to the stored stereotype. Why we do that? The answer is simple; the mind is lazy by nature, and does not want to investigate every event or person we see, whether the accusation is valid or not. The stored cultural materials in our unconscious mind are like an autopilot, influencing us without our awareness. This is why living in an oppressive culture can be dangerous to the human soul, because we internalize the experiences and they become part of our psyche.

The conscious mind cannot store large volumes of information or observations for a long period. Thus, it keeps sending information or observations to store in the unconscious mind. Without investigation of the validity of such information, the unconscious mind accepts the information wholesale, never looking into whether this information is helpful or not. On the contrary, the unconscious mind takes the negative information and exaggerates it to the degree that it scares the individual. We call that the sly mind and its job is to protect us, not to make us happy. Thus, any shred of information that comes to the conscious mind will be sent to the unconscious mind for storage, and to keep it raw, and try to bring it forward when it is needed, or when circumstances require.

Therefore, culture works to provide the individual with conclusions about almost anything. Consequently, it takes away creativity and spontaneity. In other words, culture makes us a pawn, moving us in any direction it likes. Culture plants prejudice and bias in us. Culture also justifies the use and abuse of others, and is cruel in its judgment.

Not all culture is negative, however. There are also wonderful qualities about culture. For example, culture reinforces positive attitudes, or encourages people to be helpful to each other, or to have social responsibility.

The culture of power and male domination. Throughout human history, man has had a strong desire to dominate women, even in the remote tribes of Africa. It is not necessary that man be stronger than woman. Instead, man feels inferior to woman. He feels female sexuality can challenge him in the bedroom, and he feels very inadequate or vulnerable. His vulnerability may push him to compensate for his sexual inferiority by being domineering over women. This is all attributable to man's sexual inferiority. The man has a penis, and it has to be erect. If he is anxious, it will not be, and that threatens his manhood. The female sexual organ is far superior to the males. This is why a man tends to abuse women: he is fearful of her. Unconsciously, she castrates him. It is such an embarrassment to man that his penis, the organ of pleasure, may become the source of his disturbance.

Women, on the other hand are in a much better position than man. Her sexual organ is inside and not noticeable. If she has no desire for sex, she can fake it. Masters and Johnson reported that 85% of American woman fake orgasms. When she fakes it, no man is skillful enough to find out. Women can make the sexual act close to real, and a man can believe it, and she can get away with it. Therefore, in order for the man to compensate for his sexual inferiority, he has to demonstrate domination over the woman. In reality, it is not domination; it is rather compensation for his sexual inferiority. Once a woman understands this complex sexual concept, she does not need to be upset over the gender imbalance in society, or over the domination of man.

The other part of pseudo-domination is that men earn more money than women. But the crux of the matter is, the power is not in earning, it is in spending. A woman tends to spend three times more than a man. Two thirds of American malls are designated for women's merchandise. Thus, overtly, we say man is dominating, but covertly women are the ones who dominate. They have the finances to spend and relieve anxiety.

Woman is God's final creation. Interestingly enough, when God created the universe, the last creature created was woman. Thus, she was created almost perfect, with no flaws. This is why she feels more depressed than man. She feels guilty that man is struggling with his own imperfection and she sympathizes, and feels depressed over his condition. Her depression can also be explained in two other ways: either she feels she is living with an imperfect creature, or she feels human enough to give him the feeling that she is struggling as well. Is there also another facet of man domination? Woman convinced man that he has to be in front of any danger to protect her. Therefore man puts himself in danger just to prove to her that he is a worthwhile creature. Furthermore, he may sacrifice his life for his woman. Rarely do we see the opposite, because woman is a narcissistic creature.

Culture has twisted our attitudes toward the opposite sex, and the battle of the sexes has been marketed as something important. In reality, it is not important, because society needs both of us, each one serving a different function. The promotion of the difference between men and women basically has economic reasons. When we split from each other, we need more refrigerators, stoves, or furniture. Thus, in a market economy, we have to promote our differences rather than our completion of each other. John Gray's book, *Men Are From Mars, Women Are From Venus*, is basically for commercial use. Man and woman are from the same clay; they need each other to make a family or to live a productive life together. However, there are differences between the two, and this is quite fine, just as we differ with our brother and sisters. We do not need to make an issue out of it. In reality the beauty is in our differences. Imagine if we were all similar to each other. What a boring world that would be! Helen Fisher put it eloquently: **man and woman are like two feet; they need each other to walk.**

Sadly enough, We like to create drama, and capitalize on negativity. The exaggeration of negativity is a real part of the human mind. Why? It came to us through the evolution of millions of years. We survived the harsh life, and the predators that attacked us. Thus, the events of the past have shaped our conscious mind, and we carry it from generation to generation throughout human evolution. This is why we have to be very careful of what elements of our culture we store in our mind.

The other part of the cultural domination of men is, we are aggressive by nature. We have to have an object of our hostility. Men find women as an easy target of his hostility. Why? The fear of castration; the domination is out of fear, not just power. Once we understand the psychology of both sexes, it becomes clear why such domination exists. It is an inner dynamic rooted in our unconscious mind. But, it is not as simple as men dominating women. Culture has created this scenario as face-saving device for men, because of his inherent sexual vulnerability to women. A close examination of the concept of man domination shows it is the complex dynamic of sexuality between men and women. One feels superior, and the other feels inferior. Although we call this domination, it is merely a reaction to fear.

The collectivist culture and individualistic culture. Most of society is collectivist;, western culture is individualistic. Western culture values the independent over the interdependent, focusing on distinction rather than continuation. For example if you ask an American and a Japanese to describe the fish in the sea, the Japanese describes the surroundings, while the American describes the large fish, showing that Americans focus on the individual fish, while the Japanese focus on the surroundings and the small fish. According to psychologist Richard Nesbit, there is a difference in the way people think. In the West, it is analytical. In the East it is holistic. This is how people conceptualize themselves. Western culture emphasizes individuals as unique entities, while Eastern culture emphasizes the individual in relation to other people and their environment.

Most would agree that culture can have a large influence on our daily lives: what we wear, say, find humorous. Culture also affects how our brain responds to different stimuli. There are advantages and disadvantages to both cultural perspectives.

The individualistic culture promotes creativity, and tends not to pass judgment on others; it takes people the way they are. It is also free and values individual freedom highly. But, in the individualistic culture, the individual feels lonely, because he has to fend for himself. The individual derives his identity from his own merits, not from others such as family, tribe or organization.

In the collectivist culture, the individual may derive his identity from the group, family, tribes, or from organizations to which he may belong. It is not from his earnings, or his own accomplishments. The positive side of this is, the individual has the sense of belonging and the sense of community. But at the same time, it hinders individual creativity, and makes the individual slave to the judgment of the group. It makes him a person who seeks approval of others, and that interferes with his own concept of being fully independent. Thus, each culture has advantages and disadvantages, which can either facilitate individual growth, or hinder it. My own biases are that western culture facilitates human growth, and is more suitable for modern times. With the advancement of communication and technology, there is no place for an individual who relies on his people or tribe to shape his identity.

The hegemony of culture. Often, culture wants us to have an identical appearance, not to have an individual differentiate himself from others. Again, with advancement of communication, culture is becoming less effective in shaping people. Culture used to have a strong grip on people, but no longer. Now, thoughts and ideas can travel fast to any part of the world, and can affect a person who lives in Magnolia, for example. The world is becoming a small village, and we influence each other. We are shaping each other's perspectives, through the internet and Facebook, and the smart phone. It is an incredible evolution that brought people closer, and at the same time, distance has increased between us. It is a paradoxical trend.

Often, culture plays a major role in self-alienation. A person disowns himself to be part of the culture. Culture is designed to alienate individuals for the sake of the majority. Thus, we have to liberate ourselves from the tyranny of culture. As Sartre said, "others are hell." When you differentiate yourself, you upset the balance of the culture.

Today we suffer from the hegemony of the planet's culture; the depressed man in Brazil may influence the psychology of people in Morocco. Because, metaphorically speaking, there is no difference between you and me; there is a collective consciousness. What goes in me may go inside of you. As Deepak Chopra said, we metabolize all of our experiences. Our daily experiences are a collection of one conscious mind. Before this advancement, there was a separation between people, but now it is very hard to separate oneself from others.

Mankind is becoming more anxious and fearful as a result of the rapid advancement in technology, and our brain is no longer able to comprehend progress that fast. Thus, depression increases, and we become more anxious, with episodes of panic attacks. Our brain has been designed to survive in the savanna, hunting and gathering, not for such incredible advancement in many areas of our life. The aim of the individual today is to liberate himself from the bonds of culture and modern technology, which stifling our creativity and spontaneity.

The rational question that presents itself now is, why do we feel proud when we are born in a certain culture? What does that culture has to offer to us, besides making us part of the herd? It is the ultimate human stupidity that we feel proud of something we did not choose to be. If the accident of birth brought me to be born in Japan or Germany, why feel proud of Japan or Germany, which l did not choose as my place of my birth? Culture can lock up the individual in stupid practices. It enslaves people. We see that very clearly in the Indian culture, which segregates people into classes and castes, and no one dares to cross from one to another, even in marriage. People blindly adhere to this cultural practice, and become slaves to their meaningless cultural practices.

If we dig deep into the human psyche, we discover the roots of our obedience to cultural practices stems from our hidden unconscious desire to be dominated. Domination can have many forms. It often takes the form of religion, a political system, an organization, or even identifying with dictators or despots. We cannot stand to be free individuals, because that may cause anxiety. This is why, often, we seek our enslavement, whether it's cultural or otherwise. Nevertheless, Krishnamurti, the Indian philosopher, said "do not be well-adjusted to a sick society."

Chapter Nine

The Psychology of the Sheep Mentality

As we have seen, human nature is corrupt, and one of the salient features of corruption is, we like to dominate other people. In other words, we like to enslave people, as well as be dominated ourselves. We like to take advantage of people, and manipulate others. We abuse others, mainly the disadvantaged, the weak, or the fragile. You may think, are we that bad? Yes, we are bad and often not decent creatures. We need to understand what is behind this corrupt nature.

Domination. We have a hidden sadistic tendency: we enjoy inflicting pain on others. Somehow, this gives us a thrill. Where does this come from? Perhaps from the pain we encountered in childhood, or the disappointment we have in our lives. It could also be an innate desire to cause pain to others, maybe as a result of low self-esteem. Furthermore, abusing others gives us power over them, and therefore we feel good about ourselves. The abused person needs an abuser, and normally the abused have masochist tendencies, and like to be abused. Just as the tango needs two people to dance, the sadistic individual needs the masochist in order to perform their dance. The dynamic can be very subtle. It may take a professional psychologist to recognize such a dance in human behavior.

People like to increase their power. We also like to be abused; the abuser molds the victim to become reliant on the abuser for love, affection, money, home or whatever. The victim and the victimizer need each other. The victim has a low self-concept, so they latch onto any love shown them. If we look at human nature, we find most of people suffer from an underlying psychological disorder.

For example, throughout history man has oppressed woman, and that stems largely from man's desire for power and control, as well as the fear of castration by woman. These same needs throughout human history have driven man to try to conquer and subjugate others, and to oppress classes or groups in his own society. Since man feels the need to gain as much power and control as he can, he tries to increase his sense of significance, status, and the sense of indispensability over fellow humans. Often, people internalize the oppression of the thoughts, attitudes, feelings and behavior of the oppressor toward themselves.

The other part of our corrupt nature is identification with the aggressor. When we encounter persistent aggression, we feel helpless. We need to change our helplessness to feel more powerful; the shortest method is to identify with the sources of aggression toward us. Once we do that, it will give us a relief from our sense of weakness. The tyrant, despot, or dictator use this particular human tendency to maximum effect and people become the object of his hostility. Once this identification takes place, there is another stage of indoctrination, which tyrants implant in people's minds, that the tyrant is better than sliced bread. Sadly, the human mind accepts this without question, because we cannot bear feeling weak or abused. That constitutes a threat to the ego, and we always try to keep our ego in a safe place through such pathological identification.

Also, we are lazy by nature, and this laziness contributes to our slave mentality. Often, we do not like to take responsibility; we like to be part of the herd. Taking responsibility can be very challenging. Dictators are aware of this human weakness and they take advantage, to control people. People may still feel safe if someone is controlling them, and they do not like to face life alone. This is why we often seek our enslavement by ourselves. There is comfort in being a slave; someone is taking care of you and there is no need to think for yourself, even if you are being controlled. The mind does not like to be challenged; it is lazy and seeks comfort, even under a tyrant who inflicts abuse.

Humans seek their own suffering and pain; that is a property of self-worth, or self-appreciation. If someone values himself, he does not wish to expose himself to pain and suffering. But when you do not value yourself, you attract all the negative energy in the world. If we investigate this particular aspect of human pain, we find it all is self-inflicted or self-manufactured pain. Often, the most painful thing we put in our head is fear and doubt about ourselves.

The psychology of the slave. Normally slaves have specific characteristics. They tend to be obsequious, they ingratiate themselves with other people, and they lie. They tend to be abusive to people below them, and obsequious to the people above them, because they believe in their master. They do not believe in God. They may say they do, but they do not. Once you have a deep belief in the Almighty God, there is no need to be weak, because God wants you to be strong. There is no need to lie, because God grants you what you have to have in life. In Arabic it is called Razek; you are supposed to have what you have as far as income; God is the one who feeds you. It is a very soothing submission.

Unfortunately, we are trained to be slaves by the educational system, family system, social system, and religious system, as well as the government. All are channeled toward the slave mentality, wittingly and unwittingly, because it is easy to manage slaves, and difficult to manage free men. Slaves also make life difficult for themselves and other people around them, because their dysfunction can be a hindrance. Dysfunction breeds dysfunction; this is the chain we see in the Arab world, even where there are educated people. The Arab world has many educated people, but they tend to be lay people, and their education does not help society at all. The whole Arab system is geared toward serving the slave mentality. Innovation and creativity are not encouraged, because that will constitute a threat to the slave mentality.

People in the Arab world, throughout hundreds of years, are used to this way of living; it is almost the norm to be a slave. Undoubtedly, there are free men, but they have to leave; most immigrate to the West. The oppression can be very overwhelming, and they cannot stand it. Thus, they have to leave, so those left in the Arab world are the people who have no means to leave, and the ones who accept the slave lifestyle.

There can be another form of slavery, whereby we are owned by a system, a machine, government, religion, our children, or by any power that influences us to do what it wants. Often, many people do not realize they are slaves. For example, they work hard to put their kids in school, then are slaves to their children. Or they buy a shiny new car, putting them in debt. But the most enslavement we put ourselves in, is the fulfillment of our biological needs by getting married and having children. You can also be a slave to the rat race, or to fame. Being a slave or being part of the herd can be the unconscious desire to be accepted and counted, and you may sacrifice your own dignity just to be part of the organization.

Certain cultures promote the liberty of mankind, not willingly but forcefully, by designing laws that protect human freedom. But, there are cultures that encourage enslavement or encourage people to be submissive and docile. In other words, the culture forces people to be slaves and walk with the herd without question. Clearly, the Arab culture does not promote the creativity or dignity of people. The institution of religion dominates Arab lives, keeping all people in check. The practice of religious rituals, does not add anything to religion. We all know that, but keep repeating them over and over, until we become slaves to these rituals themselves.

The slave mentality is not specific to one person, thing, place or memory. The most dangerous situation is to be a slave to the chronic persistent thoughts that keep coming to our mind, making us miserable. For instance, the thoughts of anxiety, fear, or obsession all have a dynamic of their own and truly make us slaves without our admission. That is true enslavement; we are helpless and hopeless when it comes to such persistent thoughts, which push us to practice certain rituals. You resist them, you abhor them, but these thoughts keep coming. You are a slave to your sly mind.

The hardest challenge we have to face is to free ourselves from our inner enslavement; our thoughts, fears, and the illusion of self. The second challenge is to free ourselves from cultural bondage, which has designed rules for us to follow. Often, these rules stifle our soul and turn us into robots that society controls. A third challenge is related to the previous one: how to free ourselves from the influence of others' judgment. That can be the ultimate challenge; to be independent of the good and bad judgment of others. To take others opinions with a grain of salt requires self-confidence, courage, inner security, a positive self-image, and an understanding of the motives of people.

All what we have mentioned in this chapter has two purposes. The first is to understand the dynamic of the herd mentality and second, the hidden desire within many people to be dominated by someone else. That gives psychological comfort and freedom from shouldering responsibility but people need to be aware of the insidious disorder of being a slave.

Chapter Ten

Everybody wants to go to heaven, but no one wants to die:

Why Do We Resist Change?

Change liberates us from our distorted self, as the Indian philosopher Krishnamurti said. Before we talk about change, we need to learn about us. How are we? We are creatures of habit and routine; we need a clear understanding of habit formation before we delve into change and why we resist it. Our brain is an incredible and very complex, evolving machine. We have numerous needs. For example, we need to eat. We are social creatures; we like to chat with one another. There are myriad behaviors that are just as complicated, if not more so. How on earth do we get all of this done? Habits come in, and help us through our days. For example, consider making yourself breakfast. Your behavior and movements become stereotyped, and the same with many behaviors. You may not always like your behavior, though. Sometimes your behavior can be displeasing to you.

When you do not like your behavior, then you resolve to change your undesirable behavior or bad habits. Often, you may succeed, but often you fail miserably. Not because you are a weak person, but because habits are very hard, extremely hard, to change. They are ingrained in our unconscious mind. They become automatic behaviors, coming out even if you are not thinking about them. In reality, habits take over our entire lives and we may basically become helpless in the face of habits. Some habits turn into addiction, and that can be extremely hard to tackle and overcome. Therefore, we need to be very mindful of any behaviors we engage in repeatedly.

What is the point of having a habit which does not free your mind, but rather can shackle your creativity? What is the point if you become a slave to your own habits? A creature of habit has a brain that is on autopilot, making decisions through automatic response. Habits are easy options; it is easier, through habit, to embrace an action that makes us comfortable, instead of disrupting our daily routines. Habits come from repetition; what we did yesterday, we will do today, (whether it is positive or negative), and what we will do tomorrow.

The world's behaviors have changed the place we live, and to a large extent, for the worse. For example, eating habits have resulted in an epidemic of obesity, travel habits have resulted in climate change, and consumption habits have resulted in economic recession.

Habits are funny things. We reach for them mindlessly, the unconscious comfort of familiar routines. As William Wordsworth put it, "no choice, but habits rule the unreflecting herd". Brain researchers have discovered that when we consciously develop new habits, we create parallel synaptic pathways. The more new things we try, the more we step outside of our comfort zone, the more inherently creative we become, both in the workplace and in our personal life.

The inconvenience of change. Thought leads to action.... action leads to habits....habits become characters ....characters determine our destiny. That is our eternal life. We are creatures of habit; we find comfort in regularity. When something out of the ordinary comes along, it forces us to dig deep and make a u-turn instead of continuing straight on. Change is inconvenient, because it is connected to our brain and psyche.

It is not because some people have willpower and others do not. Killing old habits is hard; once those ruts are worn into the hippocampus, habits are ingrained into us. As Aristotle said, "we are what we repeat."

Our society has conditioned us that the unknown in life can be dangerous. The very anatomy of change is determined not by your surroundings, but by your inherent mindset. Our brain finds it hard to mentally morph and glide with change. But change is inevitably happening around us, even if we are not conscious of it.

The value of habit formation.

⅄ Habits provide structure and discipline to our lives.
⅄ Habits allow us to get things done, even the mundane stuff.
⅄ Habits give you a result for being consistent.
⅄ You feel good about yourself, spread that to other people.

Sometimes, we become so used to routines that we rarely stop to question what we are doing. Doing repetitive things everyday without questioning can make us stagnant. Our brain starts to rely too much on our unconscious behavior, which prevents us from seeing all the choices available to us.

It takes us about 20 years to develop our personality. During that time, we develop habits and behavior which stay with us for the rest of our lives. Some of these habits and behaviors are not healthy or helpful to us. Some even cause serious difficulties in life and in our relationships. Since behavior is developed over a long period, it takes an equal amount of time to unlearn the behavior. You cannot wake up in the morning and say "I am going to drop such behaviors." Once our minds know that, there will be a great resistance. Our mind does not like change, even if the habit or behavior is painful. The brain conforms to what we feed it, and once we decide to drop something, then we will be faced with incredible resistance.

The definition of habits. A habit is behavior repeated in a consistent context, incrementally increasing automatically. Habitual behavior tends to lack awareness, be unintentional, uncontrollable, or done without thinking. <u>First we make our habits, then our habits make us.</u> Habits are subtly woven into the fabric of everyday life, and etch themselves in our neural pathways, because of the plasticity of our brain, and how society affects our nervous system. As is said, it is easier to reform anything except our own habits.

Does changing habits get more difficult as we get older? Yes, because we become more comfortable and familiar in our lives. Our lives are the sum of our behavior, thoughts, feelings and actions, which we have learned and incorporated into our lives. Habits are very difficult to change at any age, because people do not like to change a familiar behavior with an unfamiliar one; it can be scary and people tend to avoid fear. Making lasting changes in behavior is rarely a simple process, and usually involves a substantial commitment of time, effort, and emotion. Whether you want to lose weight, stop smoking, or stop obsessive thinking, there is no single solution that works for everyone. There is a process known as the Stages of Change Model, but first we have to understand the elements of change:

- Readiness to change -- do you have the resources and knowledge to successfully make a lasting change?
- Barriers to change -- is there anything preventing you from changing?
- Expecting relapse -- what might trigger a return to the former behavior?

We are afraid of change. Change freaks us out, but it is an amorphous issue that we do not think about. It manifests itself subtly in so many ways. But when we fail to change, our own emotional immune system is covertly at work, defending us from false perceived threats, or sometimes we sabotage ourselves.

When someone's concept of reality is challenged, there is the prospect of losing the ground on which they base their life. When someone gives you a new idea, you instantly, consciously or not, tend to reject it, because you always yearn for your own comfort zone. However, change is a basic thing in life. Those who have new ideas always shake up other people, who prefer to stay in their circle of comfort, instead of exploring the unknown.

The definition of change. Change refers to modifications or replacement of behavior. Change has a considerable psychological impact on the human mind. To the fearful it is threatening, because it means things may get worse. To the hopeful it is encouraging, because things may get better. To the confident it is inspiring, because the challenge exists to make things better. (King Whitney, Jr.)

Know thyself. Despite our best attempts to know ourselves, the truth is we know astonishingly little about our own mind, and even less about the way others think. As Charles Dickens put it "a wonderful fact to reflect upon, that every human creature is constituted to be that profound secret and mystery to every other."

Psychotherapy: the model of change. Modifying uprooting old habits can be painful. Take time to reflect on what really bugs you about you, and you may come up with a list of many things. Trying to delete a habit from your mind by yourself can be a difficult task. In such a case you may need professional help. We have a multi-million dollar industry which caters to self-help, and many workshops teach people to change. But the depression rate is on the rise, and people are more anxious. All professional psychology is about helping people to make and sustain successful change in their behavior, or to prevent negative thinking; to solve, or at least alleviate, problems. But the problem with people when it comes to change is not a lack of information, but lack of motivation. People arrive at different stages of readiness for change, and we should know how to tailor our approach accordingly. The individual may learn or strive to accept what is, as opposed to dwelling on what he thinks it ought to be. A great place to start change is getting rid of the habit of defining yourself based on external factors, or the approval of others.

There is no magic pill that makes you happier, or turns you into a better person, or solves your problems. The scientific approach works by redirecting the stories we tell about ourselves and the world around us, with subtle prompts, in a way that leads to a lasting change; in other words, editing your story. There are many stories we tell ourselves unconsciously that will affect us deeply in our thinking and behavior. Timothy Wilson, a social psychologist who came up with a fascinating approach, asks people to write their current stories, the one that influences their behavior. Then they come up with an alternate story, and figure out a way to expose themselves to this new story. The new story is adopted, and behavior changes radically and permanently.

The method came from Aristotle, who went about cultivating virtue. In our ceaseless quest for self-improvement and our relentless pursuit of happiness, we need to see the method that propels our progress, rather than derailing it. Wilson sees that what is true of the culture is also true of the individual. Our experiences in the world are shaped by our interpretation of it. The story we tell ourselves can often become distorted and destructive, and completely hinder our ability to live a balanced, purposeful, happy life. So the key to personal transformation is story transformation. Furthermore, story editing is a set of techniques designed to resolve people's narratives about themselves and the world, in a way that results in lasting behavior change (change narratives).

Another social psychologist, Kurt Lewin, also talks about changing the narrative. "Do good, be good." This approach dates back to Aristotle, premised on changing people's behavior first, which in turn changes their perception of the kind of person they are, based on the kind of things they do. The stories that people tell themselves are fascinating. To delve into a personal narrative can make a difference between living a healthy, productive life or not. How can we alter those narratives to enact positive lasting change? In order to change people's behavior, we have to get inside their heads and understand how they see the world. The story and narrative they tell themselves helps explain why they do what they do. The first exercise in this method is writing. We ask the person or people who wish to change to write their narratives, then ask them to revise them. Kurt Vonnegut said we are what we pretend to be, so we must be careful about what we pretend to be. It is a self-review approach. Then we write down the new narrative and initially look for small changes in story editing, which helps us with emotional health, perhaps reaping huge benefits.

A close look into human behavior and why we resist change. We all resist change. It seems the more we tell people what to do, the more we invite resistance. Significant psychological change necessarily involve struggle; change can be like freeing oneself from a self-imposed prison cell. Behavior is purposeful, but much of the purpose is unconsciously determined, and conscious fears mask partially unconscious wishes. Our mind is lazy, and people see no problems in their lives, or there can be a psychological barrier to behavioral change. When we achieve inwardly, the will to change outer reality will follow. However, most people do not want to change for the following reasons:

1. They do not have enough courage;
2. The surroundings are holding them back;
3. They have encountered few failures and they want to give up any change;
4. They do not feel enough pain to push to go through change;
5. They do not know the practical steps to change.

The basic principle for change is to develop communion, affection, and love with ourselves, so we can see ourselves in a bright light. If we see ourselves from a poor perspective, we would not be able to change. It is like losing weight. If you see yourself as an ugly, obese person and want to lose weight, then the body will hold the fat and you will never lose weight. But if you have love for your body and you would like to be healthy and have a new lifestyle, you lose weight because you are befriending your body, and the body responds to such positive attitudes.

Inner peace. We all strive to have inner peace and serenity; rarely, some of us achieve it, while the majority of us just internally live a chaotic life. To work toward having inner peace is to have acceptance of the dark and bright sides within us. We need not to look for other's approval, just have inner satisfaction and contentment. Do not give in to the demands of the ego, and most of all, stop the inner monologue. Keep the mind quiet, and do not allow chatters. Normally, mind chatter can disturb all the sense of peace within and it keeps us swirling constantly on the stage of life. Inner peace is the ultimate achievement for any person in life. Once you have it, you are in complete harmony with the whole world.

We have to reclaim our reality. We all form our own reality, and it is not a perfect one. However, our perception of ourselves and the world around us can get in the way. Because our self-perception is limited, it can shake up our notion of the world. But if we have a high perception of ourselves, it can do wonders for our productivity, creativity and happiness. As David Eagleman explained, in a literal sense, you cannot perceive much more of the world then you already do, and you only perceive what you really need in order to survive. We open our eyes, and then we think we are seeing the whole world out there, but the invisible world is beyond our vision and comprehension. And there is no doubt that the invisible world is controlling the visible world.

We need to be careful about a self-centered view. Looking at a situation from the opposite of your view can be very helpful. Alter your perception of self to expand your notion of the world. We see the world through our own set of filters, but changing those filters is no different than editing your self-perception.

Mapping your steps to change:

1. List your improvement goals;

2. Identify behavior that keeps you from your goal;
3. Discover your competing commitment in you, then list the opposite behaviors;
4. Identify your big assumptions;
5. Start to change your mind set.

The five stages of change. Two people came up with the model of change: James Prochaska and Carlo Diclements. The **first** stage is **pre-contemplation.** People in this stage tend to deny they have problems, and don't even think about change. They do not see problems; however, they may ask questions about their situation or their behavior.

The **second** stage is **contemplation.** People display ambivalence about their behavior and conflicted emotion about the problem they may face. They are aware of the values of making some changes in their behavior. In this stage they see they will give something up if they go through change, but they also see they can gain some emotional or mental stability if they change.

The **third** stage is **preparation.** They collect information about change and make a small change, or they may gather information about change and list some motivation, or find resources to encourage the change. Stage **four** is **action.** They take direct action toward achieving goals, and start to reward themselves. They refresh their commitment and believe in the ability to change. The **fifth** stage is the **maintenance** stage. The person maintains the new behavior and avoids the temptation to fall back. They avoid their former behavior, and keep the new behavior, replacing old habits with new positive ones. This model can be suitable for all types of addictions.

Steps for inner change:

1. Attention training to create a quality of mind that calm and clear (stop all the mental chatter);
2. Self-knowledge and self-mastery. Be able to observe your thought stream and the process of emotion with a high

clarity. Know the ulterior motive for your own behavior; in other words, have insight.

3. Create useful mental habits and try to think positively toward people, and   try to do so unconsciously. Change comes from the internal landscape of the mind.

If we do not change we do not grow. If we do not grow then we are really not living (Gall Sheehy). As Gandhi eloquently put it, "be the change that you want to see in the world". There is an old saying that 95% of people try to change the world around them, and only 5% try to change themselves. Sometimes, we may feel a fraud. If we are unable to radically change ourselves or our lifestyle, it is difficult to ask others to change.

When it comes to change we flip-flop between hope and despair. That can be exhausting in itself. We may be compassionate with other people but when it comes to ourselves we are not. We lack the self-appreciation which can motivate us to change and bring the best to our lives. We need to change ourselves, not our circumstances. Do the thing that you fear and the death of fear is certain. Try not to run away from the needed change in your life; face it, so the journey of life can become meaningful and enjoyable.

How to take care of your mind. The tool of change comes from our mind, and once we take good care of our mind, then we are on right track when it comes to change. We spend an exorbitant amount of time and energy, not to mention money, to take care of our bodies; we try to look and feel our best. But when it comes to the mind we pay less attention. We think our mind is out of our control when it is our lives that create our mind. There are a few habits we have to develop to cultivate our mind for less stress, more creativity, less distraction and a more enjoyable life.

Steps for the cultivation of our mind:

1. Make time for stillness;

2. Meditation;
3. Read a lot and never stop reading; it will sharpen your mind;
4. Let it be;
5. Do not sweat small stuff; it is one of the most toxic things you can do when you keep trivial things camping in your mind;
6. Flex your memory muscles;
7. Unplug and recharge;
8. Let your mind wander;
9. Linger in the positive and build daily rituals;
10. Do not exaggerate issues, and most of all;
11. Be watchful of your internal monologues, and do not let them carry you someplace you do not want to be.

An ancient text indicated: "We make a myriad of quick decisions unconsciously." We choose actions and form opinions via mental processes which are influenced by bias, reason, emotions, and memories. The challenging question is whether we really even have free will, but others believe it is well within our power to make choices that will lead to greater well-being.

Chapter Eleven

The Cult of Money and Human Greed

Money makes the world go around; everything seems to revolve around money. If not for money, people would not need to work. The world would crumble, because nothing would get done. Go to a busy street, where everyone is going to either earn or spend, money. Money is at the root of most political issues, the fuel for revolutions, and for obsession of the masses. In Hebrew, the word for money translates as intense desire.

Money is supposed to serve you, but sadly, we started to serve money. The concept of greed has several qualities: miserliness, envy, covetousness, and avarice, are all the mother and matrix of greed. It is the root and consort of all other sins. Greed motivates theft, and theft is the common thread in all the trouble people face, with most of the politicians around the world. Greed is the negative articulation of natural human motivation; it is the human conundrum of our existence. Greed is our inner companion, hoarding more than one can ever use in his life time. The translation of greed is basically self-serving; thinking only of one's self while hoarding at the expense of others.

Greed is the tendency toward selfish craving, grasping and hoarding. It is excessive desire for more than is needed or deserved, especially money, wealth, food, or possessions.

Greed is also called avarice, covetousness and cupidity. Greed generally is considered a vice, and is one of the seven deadly sins in Catholicism. Buddha regards craving as a hindrance to enlightenment, and a delusional state of seeking happiness, through acquiring money and material things.

How we define greed. Greed is the accumulation of material goods, whether needed or not. Examples include global corporate corruption, the neocolonial rape of the third world, and the imperialistic slaughter and occupation of foreign nations. The world today is saturated with injustice. Gordon Gekko said greed is not good, but self-interest is. What is the root of money? Money is a tool of exchange, which cannot exist unless there are goods produced, and man is able to produce them. Money shapes the principles of men who deal with one another. When you accept money in payment for your efforts, you do so only because of the conviction that you will exchange if for products of the efforts of others.

How the English dictionary defines greed: excessive consumption or desire for food, gluttony; excessive desire for wealth and power. Greed is infectious; Francine Morrissette said "he who dies with the most stuff wins." Greed is an overwhelming desire to have more of something than is actually needed. Money is only a tool; it will take you wherever you wish, but it will not replace you as the driver. It will give you the means for satisfaction of your desires, but it will not provide you with those desires. Money is the scourge of men who attempt to reverse the law of causality; men who seek to replace the mind by seizing the products of the mind.

Money will not purchase happiness for the man who has no concept of what he wants. Money will not give him the code of value, and will not provide him with a purpose. Money will not buy intelligence for the fool, or admiration for the coward, or respect for the incompetent. Money is only a means of survival. The verdict you pronounce upon the sources of your livelihood is the verdict you pronounce upon your life. Money is the barometer of a society's virtues.

The components of greed:

<u>Early negative experiences.</u> When a child experiences some negative feedback from his parents, or from his surroundings, he feels insecure about himself, as well as the world around him. His insecurity may push him to value money or material possessions more than usual. Early negative experiences typically consist of insufficient or inadequate nurturing in early childhood, or lack of love, which means the child may grow up in home that is cold emotionally, or with parents who are in constant conflict. That can definitely bring the adult to cling to money tightly. The experiences of our childhood can leave an indelible mark on our mind, and it is very hard to amend it in our adult life. The people who are treated harshly in their childhood may turn out to be greedy. Because of their insecurity, and they may think that holding money may bring security.

The other component of greed is the misconception about the nature of self, life, and others. What do we mean by that? People may develop a twisted concept that money can buy them everything, including happiness. Or, they may feel that no matter how much money they have, it is not enough to bring to them a sense of peace. Sadly, they may spend all their lives in constant fear, and insecurity is their companion. The other component is the maladaptive strategy to protect the self. Often, people see money as protection from the cold days, but in reality they are protecting the money, and the process of protecting the money can make them anxious and worried most of the time. This is why their misconception does not bring relief to them, but rather reinforces their anxiety. Therefore, the focus on money itself it can be a losing battle, psychologically and emotionally.

Human nature and greed. Human nature has the chameleon-like quality to change from virtue into vice and back again, in the wink of an eye. The inner forces that hold life in place are instruments of tension, swinging between courage and cowardice, faith and treachery, humility and pride. While greed poses the greatest moral challenge to our life, as they say, as the man grows older, his greed grows younger. Our modern culture echoes greed and self-interest; they dominate our way of living. Aristotle believed that acquiring money for its own sake is unnatural. The system of greed, exploitation, and social injustice is now a curse to most societies. Money is part of human nature, as both tool and drug. Our behavior toward money cannot be explained solely by its utility. It has a more addictive quality like a drug.

There is no end to human greed. Greed, at some point, can make people insane. Freud advocated that humans are motivated by sex and aggression. Ghazzali, the Muslim scholar, conversely advocates that human behavior is determined by four basic forces: **greed for food, sexual passion, passion for wealth and greed for supremacy**. He indicated that the top desire is greed for food, and when it is fulfilled the other desires come into play.

Greed for food is a destructive evil. The belly is the container of greed, and the breeding ground of disease and disaster. The proof is the obesity epidemic that plagues almost every society, but mainly the United State of America and the Gulf States (Kuwait, Saudi Arabia and United Arab Emirates). People are suffering from metabolic diseases like diabetes because gluttony for food is the norm in many societies. Food portions have increased in restaurants. People are more frustrated with the condition of the world, thus they resort to eating for comfort. It is a stupid process, as we consume too much food, then go to the hospital for bariatric surgery to cut the stomach, so we can eat less. Morbid obesity is the ultimate stupidity, costing us astronomical resources. Tons of food goes to waste, while we have millions and millions of people who are starving in many parts of the world.

With the satisfaction of the belly, sexual passion rises encourages companionship with the opposite sex. That can be a major motivating force in our behavior. It can encourage creativity and all forms of art, such as singing, playing music, writing, or even composing poetry. It is a powerful desire, which often leads us to sacrifice just to be with that person. Once we are with that person for a few years, we tend to get bored and seek another one. Our lives are in constant search for that person who fits that ideal picture in our head. We may consume our entire life in that search. This is the core of the human dilemma, and fulfillment can be very consuming in time, money and energy.

The desire for name and fame grows from greed as well, which contributes to hatred, clash of interests, pride, conceit, and all the dysfunctional behaviors that accompany fame. The three primary patterns of behavior are: greed for sex, greed for wealth and greed for honor and show. The secondary patterns, the ramifications of these primary patterns, are hatred, caprice, clash of interests, pride, ostentation, and impiety. Thus, Ghazzali, in this way, gave to the science of psychology an Islamic dimension in the real sense of the words.

Human nature is bad and good. We are just as capable of selfishness, greed, cruelty and violence as we are of selflessness, kindness, and compassion. One of the most detrimental human foibles from time immemorial is greed, labeled as one of the deadly sins. Chinese philosopher Lao Tzu said, "there is no calamity greater than lavish desire, no greater guilt than discontentment and no greater disaster than greed." If we are unable to control our desire, greed will rear its ugly head, and ravage everything we have. For any community or society to survive, it must adopt altruistic attitudes, and be willing to support each other. These attitudes need some cultivation, and it has to start from early childhood. However, modern societies encourage selfishness, because there is strong competition among people to win or have more.

Are human beings naturally greedy; is it a part of human biology that has been always shaped human life? The answer comes from the work of Stanford psychologist Brian Knutson, who used modern brain-image technology to try to associate regions of the brain with specific behaviors. In an experiment, volunteers pretended to buy and sell stocks while an MRI recorded the brain areas activated. The finding suggested a connection between activity in the pleasure centers of the brain and making a profitable stock sale, or risk-taking behavior, in hope of gain, such as in gambling. The experiment suggested that at a neurological level, our desire for money resembles our desire for sex. Our brain lusts after money, just as it craves sex.

In this interpretation, capitalist greed is biological, hard-wired by our brain's neural circuits. But this view is a high-tech version of the very old, mistaken notion that greed is part of human nature. Mirrors neurons give us glimpses of how our brains operate. We imitate others, and share the experiences of others. Further study has shown that humans have more highly developed neurons than monkeys. The true nature of human beings is the capacity to experience the feelings of others as much as our own. Rather than greed, the capacity for solidarity may be what makes us distinctly human (Hillel Cohen).

The psychology and sociology of greed. People think that greed is just an extension of the survival instinct. Like animals, people are concerned about having enough resources to survive tough times, when those resources are scarce. For example, squirrels hoard nuts for the winter, and humans hoard wealth as a guard against an uncertain future. However, human greed is inherently different. It is characterized by non-cooperation for the common good, and the realization that for the collective good, while selfish, we fear we will not get enough through cooperation.

If we want to understand the psychology of greed, we need to understand the Terror Management Theory. Humans, by virtue of their superior intellect, are uniquely capable of understanding mortality. This directly opposes our survival instinct and sense of self-preservation, to the extent that it causes subconscious terror. Terror is an unresolvable conflict that causes anxiety. We need a buffer to mediate the terror of mortality, so we cultivate self-esteem, which makes us feel we are a meaningful part of the world. It has been argued that our present culture places a high value on greed, fame, materialism, and wealth (Greenburg, 1990). When we are reminded of our mortality, we unconsciously strive to achieve the goals of this culture. So potent is the terror of our mortality, that we are blinded to the detrimental effects of our greed on others. All of this is a function of our anxiety buffer, which minimizes our death anxiety before it reaches the conscious mind.

Why are some people so stingy and selfish? The stingy person feels too insecure to give some of his money to others. In other words, a man can have a very large sum of money, yet still feel financially insecure, because he believes he does not have enough money. Another explanation is, we have unmet needs in one domain, which results in stinginess in another domain. That is why someone who always felt unloved by others might become very stingy. Feeling insecure about one area of our life might result in emotional or financial stinginess.

There is landmark research in this area. Two groups were given questions. One group's question forced them to think about money, and the other group's question did not relate to money. The conclusion of the research was the more a person thinks about money, the more likely he is to be stingy. This implies that people who love money, or who are obsessed with it, might find it very unpleasant to give it away. People think so highly of money, because money is wrapped up in self-worth and self-esteem for a lot of people.

While the basis of greed is considered biological, it has an even stronger social basis, as part of self-preservation and reproduction. For example, why do we like to play the lottery so adamantly, and why do Reno and Las Vegas attract millions of people to their casinos? Because, no matter how much it is decried, people are greedy; they want more than they have, and the more, the better. Rarely, does a person stop and think "I have enough and I do not need more". But, there are exceptional cases where people gave up their wealth and lived a very simple life. Normally, they give it up for religious reasons, but whatever the reason, it is very healthy to all to give up the complicated life of materialism. We can let other people make a living and share the planet's resources. As Gandhi said, "there is enough for everybody's needs, but not enough for human greed."

As far as greed on an international level is concerned, from my personal perspective, there are no poor countries. All of them are very rich, but human greed, manipulation, domination, and abuse rob many countries of their natural resources. Or they may have a different tragedy, in that the ego of their dictator has been inflated and there is no way to contain it. He may lead his people to wars, starvation, and all types of conflicts. The best example is the African continent, and the Middle East. They are so rich in everything but their people are so poor and some are dying of starvation, because of poor management of their natural resources.

Unrestrained greed in an individual can lead to callousness, arrogance and even megalomania. A person dominated by greed will often ignore the harm their actions can inflict on others. For example, sweat shops and unsafe working conditions are consequences of people whose personal greed overcomes their social conscience. Unrestrained greed is detrimental to society, as people attempt to find a balance between biological imperative and social necessity. There is a strong biological basis for human behavior, humans are social creatures. The societies and culture we create have a major effect on our behavior, mollifying and modifying our biological reactions. Self-preservation extends beyond the personal to the public, involving family, friends and even strangers. What may help our personal survival may help others, who may help us in return (Richard F. Taflinger).

This is why today we have to have laws to protect the weak, the vulnerable, the limited intellect person, the child, and women from the abuse of greedy men. Human nature is funny. You may see a wonderful human with a great heart gives and does not abuse others. At the same time, you will find the callous person who sucks the blood out of people. Consider the condition of immigrant workers in the U.S., the poor condition of workers in India or other countries, or the domestic servants in the Gulf States.

Selfishness, greed and human frailty. Selfishness is the most common trait one can find. If you follow Buddha, you know he left his family and earthly desires to seek enlightenment. It is important to step away occasionally from the swirling emotion and desires one encounters in daily life. It can be a non-stop parade of a greedy people in routine life. Humanity is characterized by greed and selfishness, originating from the need to protect one's self-interest. It is the selfish genes that play major roles in our daily behavior. Often, human greed takes over our entire behavior. We become motivated by greed and selfishness, and that is the conundrum of the human condition.

Religious teaching always warns us about going down that slippery slope; it is like a torpedo destroying what it hits along its way. The human community is struggling to have some sense of compassion among their members. But, the selfish genes get inside our skin and keep us distant from each other.

Why greed is such a powerful motive in our behavior. Greed is a natural human tendency. Once we allow ourselves to start down that slippery slope, our judgment becomes impaired, our ethics are compromised and our management style blinded with ambition. What drives people who are so powerful and wealthy to take a path that can lead to prison, or even death; when is enough, enough? It is the lust for power. Greed becomes destructive when you allow it to manage you, rather than you manage it.

Do we have a money disorder? Just about everyone has a complicated relationship with money. Studies show that money is the number one reason for divorce in the early years of marriage, and a common area of conflict and source of stress for couples. Financial strain reduces relationship satisfaction, worsens depression and leads to emotional problems, health difficulties, and poor work performance. This is how much money influences our behavior and judgment. A person with a reasonable sum of money can feel less tense, and relax.

Why does a person who is already rolling in money want more? Why do people whose lives are already comfortable make sacrifices in other areas of their lives, family, friendship and their own sanity, just to get more cash? Professors Stephen Lea and Paul Webley, from the University of Exeter explained in 2006 that money provokes people into all sorts of bizarre behavior that cannot be easily explained in terms of its function. Money turns out to be one of the most addictive games ever invented;

culture on its own is not powerful enough to explain the human motivation for money.

Greed is like a drug. It consumes people so completely that they cannot come out of it, no matter how much they try. People surrendering to greedy dream of money and more money. They would do anything -- cheating, scheming, backbiting and much more -- to make that extra buck. Such people always feel that money defines their status and power among their peers, and this is what creates their standing in life.

People today are absolutely controlled by their false sense of self. Their ego is never satisfied. Their endless pursuits for fame, fortune, and notoriety are typical. They do not know when to stop, trampling on everything in their way to get ahead. Their preoccupation with financial freedom has overtaken their whole purpose in life. They destroy natural resources, animals and the environment for their own greed and accumulations. Our ancestors did not pass on the genes with altruistic traits. The genes of greed are more powerful and have dominated all humans.

Money and happiness. Studies show people inhabit two separate worlds, the social and financial, and depending on which one is activated, their thoughts and behavior can change dramatically. Money can bring satisfaction, but not happiness. More money means you can have what you want and do what you want: house, cars, and vacations in Hawaii. Social scientists consistently find only a moderate relationship between having more money and being happy, and even that moderate connection might be exaggerated. In reality, money might have very little to do with happiness at all. But most puzzling is that people often seem aware, at some level, that money won't make them happy, yet they continue to work away earning money they do not objectively need.

People who earn more money do not spend their time enjoying themselves, shifting to enjoyable activities when they are rich. They instead spend their time at work, in activities likely to cause them more stress and tension. This may be because their focus is chasing after money. When people think about earning more money they probably imagine they would use the money on recreational activities. But in actuality, to earn that money, they have to spend more time at work, and commuting to and from work. In a surprising finding, higher earners were more likely to experience intense negative emotions and greater arousal during the day. We are living our lives worshipping the acquisition of money. But, almost everything tells us we should do that: television, billboards, newspapers, and other people are all screaming at us to get more money. Thus, the message has become unconscious, and we often act upon it, unaware of who is pushing us to be in the rat race. Cultural pressure translates to unconscious action in most instances.

In a nutshell, our head is crowded with thoughts of money, at the expense of other ideas. Acquiring money and status makes us feel satisfied with life, but we are convincing ourselves that satisfaction equals happiness. Unfortunately, it does not. Even though we appear to have everything, we are left feeling that something is missing, but are unable to identify what. That is simply feeling happy, right now in this moment (Kahneman, 2006). Research by Brigham Young University and William Paterson University indicated that those who draw a lot of happiness from money and possessions do not make happy spouses, compared to those who find their happiness elsewhere. Couples who say wealth is not that big a deal score about 15% better on marriage stability and other indications of relationship quality. But sadly, today's culture places too much of a premium on achievements and monetary gain as highly desirable goals.

The biggest problem we face is that we are never happy. For example if we receive a Nokia phone as a gift, we dream of an iPhone and are not happy with the Nokia. The list of our monetary desires seems endless. It may also make our lives a rat race. We keep running after money, without knowing the secret for happiness, which is having a sufficient amount of money to live a decent life, without struggle. That is the core of our happiness.

Love of money. Money is not the root of all evil, the <u>love</u> of money is. We are all driven by the insatiable itch for success, chasing that elusive gold at the end of the rainbow. Money is merely a measure of value. It is one of the tools of civilization, and can be used like a weapon, turned to evil purpose. The argument that the love of life is the root of man's evil is not valid, but greed, for example, is evil, because it is an excessive lust for those things which one likes in life. Greed precedes money, which allows us to liquidate and transfer almost anything, to make all things interchangeable, to put it all on the trading table. Thus, money becomes the manna to measure our lives, and rite becomes a material. Money is the language of man, and money is a very complex system. But it can show the true nature of people. When money is involved in evil, the evil is not in the money, it is in the hand taking it, or the hand giving it, or possibly both.

Why do we love money? You cannot eat it, drink it, or use it directly for anything. It is a poor substitute for wood when starting a fire, and yet we all work our butts off all our lives for it. Money makes the world go around. Benjamin Franklin said, "money never made a man happy, nor will it, yet the more a man has, the more he wants." Instead of filling a vacuum, it makes one. The love of money can never be satisfied. It is a hopeless love that always desires more. It is wasted energy. And more than that, it keeps our attitudes and actions in bondage.

When the love of money is present, freedom is not. The love of money consumes our time, wastes our energy, and devours our values. The passion for money is a trap which quickly swallows our heart's convictions and causes us to engage in behavior that we would otherwise avoid. The love of money fuels competition, dominated by jealousy and envy. The love of money limits our potential. The love of money attracts the love of money, and without a doubt the love of money destroys other loves.

The gender difference in the love of money. As far as the love of money is concerned, a woman tends to seek a man with more money, while a man is looking for a woman with affection. This is a sweeping statement, but it has a serious application in our daily lives and in the way we perceive the world. Why does a woman tend to seek the man with more money? The woman is the life giver; she gets pregnant and delivers a child. Throughout her pregnancy and beyond, she needs someone to help her in rearing the child. Thus, she focuses on security for her child. She is very concerned about the well-being of herself and her child. Often, security comes from having enough resources, and having enough resources means having money to manage life. This is the original motive for a woman to want a man who has money, so she can ensure the survival and security of her child, as well as herself.

As far as man is concerned, he sees having money as a sign of success and accomplishment. He is a naturally competitive creature, as well as the provider of the family. Normally, his masculinity is manifested in having a large penis, from a psychoanalytic perspective, but he also has money, houses, businesses and other achievements. Women look at such a man and see him as a good candidate for being a good caregiver and provider. A woman also looks for protection; she wants a man who takes care of her and her children in good times and bad. Therefore man may focus on having a solid financial means to attract a beautiful woman. However, his focus on money is not as sharp as the woman. He learns to be a provider, and spends the money that he makes, trying to bait a good woman to carry his children. Evolution psychology tells us a man looks for a healthy woman, with an ample bosom who is built for child-bearing, because that makes her a female who can produce healthy children.

Greed, power and principle. Greed and the lust for wealth and power are the only motivating factors for a few who use and exploit other human beings. If you ask people, "are you greedy?", all would deny it, but if you ask, "would you break the rules if it benefits you financially?", the answer might be, "how much money we are talking about?" Few people identify themselves as greedy, but learn about an ethical scandal from the news, and money will be at the core. The problem of greed is not just limited to the wealthy but is a human weakness. Most people though want money not to be greedy but out of necessity, to keep food on the table. Sadly, the desire to have more often overrides the ethical principle. People need to learn the core philosophy and resolve in their heart that they would rather lose their job than sacrifice their integrity (Mark S. Putnam).

The Greek philosopher Epicurus said, "wealth consists not in having great possessions, but in having few wants." We have to have a balanced perspective between our wants and needs, when you need something badly enough, you are likely to do anything to get it, which is a recipe for ethical disaster. If you live your life in a frantic quest for your wants, you will never be satisfied. You will miss out on all that life offers, and you will make mistakes along the way. Do you let your wants drive your ethical decisions? You need to understand the greed-centered attitude, and where it may take you.

Jesus once said, "you cannot love God and Mammon." People love money because they think it is insurance against disaster. But why do we need more or extra money, since we have enough to survive?

The demonic side of ourselves. No doubt, there are unseen forces driving mankind. Perhaps there is an evil, unforeseen force driving humanity to its own inevitable destruction. But that evil is not a separate external force, invisible in itself. We think we are too weak to fight it, so we stick our head in the sand and pretend it is not real, ignoring it or thinking we can pray it away. This evil force is deep within the hearts, minds, and the very essence of mankind. There are ample natural resources on this earth to sustain humanity for eons if those resources are protected, nourished and used for the benefit of all of us, instead of those select few who exploit them for personal gain and power.

The Pope said, "greed destroys, while money is God's gift to us to help others." Money itself is not a problem, but greed and an attachment to money cause evil and destroys families and relationships. Money is needed to bring about good things, but when your heart is attached to money, it destroys you. Jesus said, "no one can serve two masters, one can either serve God or money." The effect of greed in the world today is the inherited imperfection of all mankind, which puts us in the throes of greed.

There are numerous scams today developed for the sole purpose of greed. Whether the scam involves debt relief, home modification, credit scores or travel scams, it is all detrimental to its victims. There are many swindlers, (many of them are in Nigeria), thinking that scams are an opportunity to make fast money. Greed is an unscrupulous desire for wealth and power. It does not have a heart or concern for the damage it may cause. Greed is infectious and contaminates the world. It alienates the individual from family, friends and God. It is selfish and benefits the greedy individual only temporarily (remember whatever we sow, we shall reap). Why do we not focus our life on the positive seeds that will reap love? Material things, usually the focus of the greedy person, will come and go, but when you give and help others, this allows you to sleep soundly. And the old wisdom indicates: **the only thing that you get to keep is what you give away**. So giving is a virtue, and makes our life on the planet meaningful and more harmonious.

How to move beyond the desire of acquiring more money:

1. Try to see money as a tool to move through life. At its core, money is a bartering tool; it saves us from making our own clothes, tools and furniture.
2. Be content with either poverty or great wealth. Of course, you have to work and be motivated to improve your lot in life.
3. Avoid debt by any means. Try to buy when you have enough money and never buy things that you cannot cover financially. A borrower is a slave to his creditors; spending more money than you earn will always result in bondage to another. There is no simplicity in bondage. This is why most people who have credit cards are in bondage to the banks (Joshua Becker).

4. Learn to share. As Gandhi said, "there is enough for everybody in need, but not for human greed." Try to challenge the selfish genes within you, and be helpful to the people around you who are in need of financial assistance.
5. Remember that money comes and goes, like the tides of the ocean; money rolls in and out. Try not to develop a neurotic attachment to money. For example, a stingy individual has a neurotic attachment to money.
6. Try to work hard and make money, then make the money your servant. Never be the guardian of money, merely stashing it in the bank and looking through your bank statement to see how much it grows. At the same time, you are depriving yourself and your family from the good potential the money may offer to you.
7. Try to use wisdom in your spending, and do not be frivolous, extravagant, or a spendthrift. You have to have a balanced budget for your finances.
8. Never gamble. It is a pathological attachment to money, and you need serious therapeutic intervention to free yourself from it.

Finally, money is a tool to manage our daily life. Once we have it, our life becomes less difficult. When we do not have it, often our integrity is compromised. Arab wisdom indicates, when your pocket is empty, then your self is empty of ethics or moral principles. Sometimes if your pocket is full, you do not hesitate to abuse others to have more and more. The conclusion here is our relationship with money is very complicated. It has some pathological and emotional components. Once we become aware of our neurotic attachment to money, we can see how much worry occurs because of either having or not having money. We learned through scientific research that money will not bring us happiness, but it will bring us satisfaction. Happiness is a totally different enterprise, and I addressed it in my third book, *The Triumph Over the Mediocre Self.*

Chapter Twelve

The Industry of Health, Wellness and Illness

Simply speaking, the new paradigm of the healthcare system is not working, and in a way, has contributed to the rise of healthcare costs, as well as the rise of illness. Thus, we need a new paradigm of the healthcare system. The present system is focused on management of disease, and the treatment of symptoms. The suggested paradigm must focus on health and prevention. As they say, an ounce of prevention is worth a pound of cure! We talk about an evidence-based system; instead we have a reimbursement-based system. The system does not look to the etiology of illness, and has been over medicalized. Undoubtedly, the health system has prolonged our lives, but the astronomical cost is beyond comprehension, at the expense of other segments of services to society.

How we define health/wellness and illness. There is a sharp line dividing health from disease. Defining illness is a complex process, evolving over time. It is facilitated by advancements in science and validation by societal recognition. Health is the state of complete physical, mental and social well-being, and not merely the absence of disease, or infirmity (WHO, 1946).

Illness refers to the sociocultural context within which disease is experienced. Hence, we define sickness as a concept that combines the biomedical model (disease) with the sociocultural context of the patient (illness). In other words, sickness can be two parts: disease, which is biological and physiological malfunction, and illness, the experiences and perception of disease within the sociocultural context, including spirituality. The U.S. Surgeon General said, in 2011, "We cannot look at health in isolation. It is not just in the doctor's office. If you have a healthy community, you have a healthy individual." A study by the Rand Center for the Study of Aging determined "social contacts and family are the Number 1 factor affecting life satisfaction. Living in a health-positive society can have profound impacts on individual health and well-being.

I and We. How do we know the difference between illness and wellness? As Dean Ornesh put it, "it is simply between I and We." We all want to be well, yet many of us are ill. Some of us put on a mask for the outside world to see, while deep within we have many secret ghosts and illnesses that haunt us. Although some of these are pathological, most of them are imagined, and not real at all.

Many of us live and die, but never realize the very reason for life. If we would only understand that life is not a singular, self-centered experience, but a collective, interconnected experience, we would be giving and getting the life support we need to live a healthy and meaningful life. There is a thin line between illness and wellness. If we understand the difference between the two, we discover one of the deepest, most elusive, and highly profound secrets of life.

Good health is a fundamental right of all human beings. The prevention and eradication of illness through efficient, natural curative treatment would put the current health system out of business. Illness is when you live within your own selfishness, while wellness is when you get out of yourself and be available to others. Being connected to others can bridge self-separation, which can bring pain to us. Thus, wellness is all about We, and illness all about I, which can leave the individual in a lonely place. The human soul always seeks to be reunited with other souls. The truth is, we all want to love and be loved. If we achieve that in our lifetime we would live in a perpetual state of wellness.

Wellness is more than being free from illness. Wellness is a dynamic process of change and growth. There are many interrelated dimensions of wellness: physical, emotional, intellectual, spiritual, social, environmental, and occupational. Each dimension is equally vital in the pursuit of optimum health. Social wellness means to perform social roles effectively and comfortably, and create a support network. Occupational wellness involves enjoying your occupational endeavors and having your contribution appreciated. Physical wellness is to maintain a healthy body and seek medical care when needed. Intellectual wellness is to have an open mind when you encounter new ideas. Emotional wellness is marked by understanding feelings and coping with stress.

Existential medicine. Illness has existential causes rather than just biological causes. However, there is a total monopoly by the medical profession and its institutions, on knowledge of the body and of illness. Dr. Hence Illich in his book indicated the medical establishment has become a major threat to health. The disabling impact of professional control over medicine has reached the proportion of epidemic. The monopoly of the biomedical model is sustained, despite the plethora of alternative or complementary forms of medicine that continue to spring up as a part of the global health industry. Vitamins treatment, herbal/ homeopathic medicine, integrative medicine, energy medicine, Ayurveda medicine, or traditional Chinese medicine are all wonderful tools to be used to restore wellness to the body. Sadly, the medical establishment often has only a hammer; thus, they treat everything as if it were a nail.

The concept of death. Why do we prolong life? We are faced with the growth of our elderly population, because the medical advancement has done marvelous things to postpone death. However, we should not be fearful of death. As Steve Jobs, the founder of Apple Computer, put it eloquently, <u>death is the best invention of life.</u> We need to focus on the quality of life. How can we live a healthy lifestyle, make our life meaningful, and prevent illness before it happens? If we reach a condition where illness takes over, and the quality of our life is no longer enjoyable, or we are in perpetual pain, then we should have the right to end life by any means (euthanasia). We should not involve morality in the management of our illness and pain. It has to be a very personal decision, up to the individual who suffers. If the individual is unaware of his existence (unconscious), then his family or another caregiver may be involved. We also need to understand that death is not the end of life; it is the beginning of new life, or in better words, a transformation. The other life may be better than what we have right now. No shedding of tears, and grieving; it is a celebration, and challenges our selfish motive to keep the sick patient in perpetual pain.

The role of pharmaceutical companies. The pharmaceutical industry has an incredible hold over the healthcare system, because it tends to define illness, then develop a drug for it, then manufacture and sell the drug. Supposedly, defining illness is <u>not</u> their mission. Unfortunately, there are several indicators that the industry is contributing to the definition of illness. Are these contributions beneficial to the good of society and ethically sound, or are they solely amid at maximizing corporate profits? Perhaps the answer to this question is painful, as the pharmaceutical can manipulate most aspects of illness and health for their own selfish motives.

The pharmaceutical companies make billions every year by perpetuating a culture of disease and illness. They exaggerate conditions, then offer their solution as the only viable treatment. I am sure a large number of doctors or health professionals are noble people who act with some sense of moral accountability, but many more are caught up as cogs in a crooked system. The same system that sees selling pills as more important than being truly healthy. A rising tide of curing diseases by prescription is turning society into one big hospital. It is time for people to reclaim their health (Jorg Blech). Illness is becoming an industrial product, and health a state that nobody can live up to anymore.

Dr. David Henry in his article, *Mongering Commentary*, in BMJ (formerly the British Medical Journal), says the pharmaceutical industry is really the selling sickness and disease industry, and pharmaceuticals have medicalized any risk factors. Much money can be made from healthy people who believe they are sick. Pharmaceutical companies sponsor diseases, and promote them to consumers who buy into their concepts. The social construction of illness is being replaced by the corporate construction of disease. They medicalize almost every aspect of our lives. They may have honorable motives, but they orchestrate and fund consumer groups to promote the use of their medications.

In an article by Doug Bandow in *Forbes,* June 2012, he notes that under the Monopoly of the FDA and drug companies, the U.S. pharmaceutical industry profits an average 18.5% of revenue, compared with 2.2% for the rest of the Fortune 500 (*Fortune* magazine, April 2002). It has been repeatedly shown that doctors' prescribing habits are influenced by interaction with industry representatives and attendance at drug company-sponsored events. The industry invested $15.7 billion in marketing in 2000. The research is heavily regulated, and does not follow international standards, or an agreed-upon clinical practice, nor does it address patient safety. Drug firms now control most of the process of clinical trials, from design and implementation through data analysis and publication (Bodenheimer, 2000). The results of these studies give an exaggerated view of a drug's benefits, but fail to publish any negative results of use of the drug. The problem is not only manipulating the result, it's also commercial pressure, which increases the risk of methodological bias and misleading reporting. In Bodenheimer's investigation, 6 out of 12 clinical investigations are blocked from publication, or altered by the drug firm.

In 1950, pharmaceutical companies helped promote pathology in children by marketing stimulants. Ritalin, produced by Ciba Pharmaceutical, is now an epidemic of stimulant use among school age and young children. Neglect of the adverse effects of drugs represents a major public health problem, with recent estimates indicating 1.5 million Americans are hospitalized and 100,000 die each year, making drug- related adverse effects one of the leading causes of death (Lazarou and Pomeraz, 1998). Moreover, 51% of drugs approved have serious adverse effects that are not detected prior to approval (U.S. General Accounting Office, 1990).

Psychiatric drugs. As a society we are consuming more medical drugs than ever, and a large proportion of those is for psychological conditions and complaints, making a major contribution to spiraling healthcare costs and taking money away from other health services. The current extent of drug companies' influence has threatened the integrity of psychiatry, and some suggestions have been made about steps that could be taken to address such violations. Mental or psychological problems are a complex entity and social problem, but often, we seek simple solutions, like seeking a "pill for every ill". Unfortunately, drugs are the central focus of treatment in modern psychiatry. When modern medication was introduced in 1950, it was considered to have crude effects.

The mental illness industry is medicalizing normality. In 2000, the WHO named depression as the fourth leading contributor to the global burden of disease, and predicated by 2020, it will rise to second place. A new survey from the European College of Psychopharmacology, a meta-analysis of a mass of earlier research, reports that a staggering 164.8 million Europeans, 38.2% of the population, suffer from a mental disorder in any year. As well as depression, this includes neural disorders such as dementia and Parkinson's, childhood problems from ADHD to conduct disorders, and anxiety disorders, from panic attacks to obsessive–compulsive disorder to shyness.

Depression and anxiety are disproportionately women's ailments. Men, it seems, become alcoholics rather than depressed. Such reports are worrying. They draw attention to a rising toll of human suffering. Women are having greater susceptibility, thus they visit doctors often, while men go to bars to drink, to medicate his depression. Humans are suggestible creatures, and doctors like to help. But they provide the pills that the pharmaceutical company recommends. Research has shown that placebos can work just as well, with fewer side effects. Society may trust the doctors to be the guardians of our well-being, but often the doctor has one tool, a hammer, and tends to treat everything as if it were a nail.

Dr. Joanna Moncrieff, in her book *Psychiatry for Sale*, indicated that worldwide, people are consuming a large quantity of prescription drugs and many of these are for psychiatric complaints. Psychiatrists have become an important target for the large and powerful pharmaceutical industry. Drug companies direct lavish advertisement and hospitality toward psychiatrists, and provide funding for medical education and mental health services initiatives. The industry is now heavily involved in the organization of research into psychiatric drugs and the dissemination of research funding. This raises questions about the scientific objectivity of this research and the extent to which the industry is able to shape the research agenda. They also exert influence at a political level, through lobbying and direct funding of political bodies, including drug regulatory agencies, and may compromise the health of patients.

The Diagnostic and Statistical Manual of Mental Disorders. The DSM is a useful tool for statisticians, and is also useful to public health administration, insurance companies, lobbying bodies, or pharmaceutical companies, who need a homogeneous population on whom to carry out drug trials. But this does not give relief to patients. Sadly, we are inventing disorders and adding more diseases to the list. Dr. Mercola indicated in his article that DSM 5 is out, and it seems we are turning healthy people into the mentally ill. We label healthy people with mental conditions, and make them prime candidates for unnecessary prescriptions of mind-altering antidepressant and antipsychotic drugs.

Virtually none of the mental disorders described in the DSM5 can be objectively measured by empirical tests. Instead, they are completely subjective by turning normal emotion and difficult life circumstances into illness. The DSM5 has resulted in rampant over–medicalization and over–diagnosis of mental illness within the psychiatric profession. For example, the bereavement after the death of a loved one now can be labeled as Persistent Complex Bereavement. Since 2.5 million Americans die each year, the number of those experiencing grief as a result is far higher. This is the market the pharmaceutical industry stands to gain, by labeling normal human emotions as psychiatric disorders, and then medicating them.

Writing a prescription is faster than engaging in behavioral or lifestyle strategies change, because it is a more lucrative approach for the conventional model. Human emotion is very difficult to test empirically. Therefore, the decision among the psychiatrists is to decide about a single illness in a vote by a psychiatrists panel; essentially making up diseases to fit the drugs, not the other way around.

Where is the art of healing and the basic health truth? The art of healing has not led to any real breakthroughs for decades. The exploitation of the national Medicare system and private insurance is rampant. These companies are guilty of the theft of people's most precious possession -- their health. We are set up to become a population of invalids, incapacitated by imaginary illnesses. What can be done to stop this? One of the answers is setting up a separate agency in charge of controlling the medicalization of disease. It should be independent and armed with a great deal of knowledge about the natural course of life. People may discover something reassuring: they are healthier than they think.

We have to understand that quality nutrition is key to good health. As the father of western medicine, Hippocrates said, "let your food be your medicine." Food is the fuel of both body and mind. If the fuel is inadequate or of poor quality, or contains some toxicity, then the body and mind will suffer. Yet, unfortunately, denial of this basic fact is very rampant within monopolistic medicine. For example, the sun is necessary for the production of vitamin D, and sadly it has been demonized, with a resultant epidemic of rickets in children. Rickets is a disease with one cause -- lack of vitamin D.

The epidemic of obesity. If we observe what has happened to our bodies in last two decades, we have to be ashamed. Obesity is an epidemic worldwide, particularly in America and the Gulf States like Kuwait, Saudi Arabia and United Arab Emirates. Sadly enough, we gorge ourselves with too much food and then we invented bariatric surgery to staple or cut our stomachs. Needless to say, bariatric surgery has many unfavorable consequences, but often people prefer an easy solution to a very complex problem, eating disorders. Instead of focusing on lifestyle change, we resort to cutting part of our body or disabling part of our stomach. In other words, we are playing with God's design.

There are many factors that contribute to our present obesity:

1. The availability of varieties of food. The food industry has become so skilled in how they present food to us, and stimulate our appetites. We are drooling over what we see in the supermarket, and that is unfair to us. Because basically we are very fragile and we cannot resist the temptations of food and sex. This is the way we are; we are motivated by the two.
2. We are bored with ourselves, and food gives us some relief from our boredom. Modern man is frustrated and suffers from existential anxiety.
3. We are depressed and seek dopamine to give us pleasure, and food can be a great source of pleasure, and can raise the level of dopamine in our brain, because we seek constant stimulation.
4. Most importantly, we seek comfort in food, which reminds us of our childhood, that mother soothed us with her milk. Now as adults, we soothe ourselves with food. We use food as a psychological comfort to ward off boredom, and spiritual emptiness.

People today are suffering from a serious case of loneliness, because of our separation from each other in spite of the advancements in communications. But we are far from each other emotionally, if not physically. Thus, food becomes the agent of comfort. Taking all these factors into consideration, we are faced with serious health problems, because obesity leads to all sorts of health problems, like diabetes, high blood pressure, high cholesterol, and various metabolic disorders. Obesity constitutes a serious health risk, not just physically, but psychologically as well. Our self-esteem suffers, and our psychic energy drains. Thus, we should focus on lifestyle change, rather than resorting to cutting part of the stomach. These are the underlying causes of obesity, so the most important step is to teach people basic skills in self-control, and find enjoyment in things other than food.

Health is a great wealth. There are many healing systems available to us today, which can be very effective in treating serious disease. Many modern healing techniques regard successful healing as the cure for physical problems, whether they are symptoms of cancer, AIDS, chronic fatigue syndrome, or some other illness. To avoid these problems, it is necessary to consider a more comprehensive view of healing that incorporates not only physical healing, but mental and spiritual healing. This is called the Holistic approach to treating ailments. This involves all the factors that contribute to the illness of the patient. We should not focus on the physical part of the illness, because the mind can play a great role in causing illness. Without a doubt, the mind is the agent of healing. We have to reach the state of ultimate healing by ridding the mind of all of its accumulated garbage[anxiety and worry].

We know that illness is an imbalanced life in many dimensions (physical, emotional and spiritual). One of the most important tenets of medicine is health and illness are not something that happens to us, it is the thinking that we do, or behavior, or our emotional reaction to events taking place in our lives. To put it precisely, sickness is the way we metabolize our daily experiences.

Also, on some occasions, the mind brings materials from the unconscious to create an illness. Why? The answer is, **illness is a conspiracy cooked in the unconscious mind, then manifested by a field trip all over the body.** Medical doctors need to be trained so the unconscious mind can be helpful in healing.

Chapter Thirteen

The Destruction of Modern Technology

We can define technology as science applied to practical purpose. However, the application of science has touched every part of our lives, whether we need it or not. Often, the side effects of the advancement of science have contributed to our restless life, and make us like squirrels; we are very nervous about the simple movements we face in daily life.

Technological advancement has been moving at the unprecedented rate. The creativity in the field of technology has resulted in remarkable innovation. We are morphing from cave man to modern man; new technology has revolutionized the way we work. Undoubtedly, modern technologies have given us unbelievable results and improved our lifestyle considerably. At the same time, we are incurring enormous disadvantages. Modern technology has replaced humans, as robots are doing the most of the jobs on production lines, which used to be done by humans. Of course, this has increased the production in different fields of business, but it has also increased the unemployment of younger workers.

This is why the youth of today are disenchanted with the whole system of production. We have moved factories to other countries where they use cheap labor, and abuse another population. The focus is on profits; whether that leads to abuse of another population is not considered. We can call it another form of slavery: economic slavery. People in less developed countries are abused and work in very dire conditions, and they earn just a little money. All this is done to satisfy our insatiable desire to have more goods, at the expense of people in less developed countries. In this situation, the souls of those people have been humiliated, as a result of modern technology.

Technology inherently breeds laziness, as jobs that were once done by people can be done by machines, and machines make our lives generally easier and require less work. Machines and factories contribute to air and water pollution across the planet, but at the same time we are addicted to modern technology, which breeds its own enormous problems. It changes and updates so rapidly that something recently bought can quickly become outdated and ineffective. In this case, technology can produce an inordinate amount of waste, and no landfill can be enough to absorb the amount of technological waste. The waste can be recycled in the western world, but in less developed countries, it is be a serious burden, and toxic to the environment.

For example, take a plastic bottle, which may take two hundred years to decompose into the ground. It produces toxicity that pollutes the ground and the air. The costs of such environmental pollution can be astronomical. We pay with our health and see the rise of diseases that result from environmental toxicity. For instance, the rate of cancer in certain spots in the world is higher, and usually it's the areas with higher pollution and toxicity. Moreover, breathing problems have increased among children around the world, because their immune system is still undeveloped and susceptible.

The dark side of technology. John Hagel indicated there is a paradox about technology: it causes mounting performance pressure, accelerating change, and growing uncertainty, all at the same time. Modern society has a staggering number of technological gizmos and mechanical gadgets at its disposal, from airplanes to iPhones. However, while these advancements have brought new aspects of health, freedom and enjoyment, there are disadvantages to a society which is completely reliant upon them. Disadvantages of technology include stress, a more hectic life, fear of nuclear war, cybercrime, higher incidence of eye diseases, increased body weight, and new transportation technology that has brought pollution and congestion to major cities.

Scientists have armed with technology that can destroy a city in a second, with the mere push of a button. Similarly, cybercrime, cheating and fraud make our life hell. The worst phase of technology is the violation of privacy by someone unknown to you, or fear of nuclear war. As they say, too much of good thing is a bad thing. We have an abundance of technological gadgets for everything you can imagine. Some are necessary, but many of them are not.

The danger of depending on technology. From day to day our world has gradually changed. The revolution of new ideas comes to the mind of every person, especially improving technology to make living better. As a result, modern technology has brought people certain advantages, like fast communications, the improvement of travel, and good healthcare. However, danger is lurking in every corner of our modern lives. Loneliness, weapons of mass destruction, pollution and the same day-to-day lifestyle are all products of modern technology.

Modern technology has made us mentally lazy. We do not use our brain, because we use tools like calculators, which reduce our creativity, as well as the challenges we face in our daily lives, which stimulate neurons. At the same time, modern technology provided us with modern war weapons, ranging from missiles to rockets to nuclear bombs. The killing of another human used to take time, using a sword or, in the example of Cain and Abel, just a rock. Now, in a matter of seconds, by the push of a button, we can kill millions and millions of people. We did this in World War II, when America dropped nuclear bombs on Hiroshima and Nagasaki. Modern technology can be very dangerous and can threaten our survival. It is clearly part of the destructive tendencies we have, as we are inherently aggressive.

Our health and modern technology. The mass production of food and the genetic alteration of food have challenged our human digestive system, because we did not evolve fast enough to compensate for the amount of processed foods we consume. Thus, new diseases are introduced, as the body is unable to adapt to the new foods and the alteration of the genetic makeup of the tomato or the watermelon. Healthcare is very progressive and vastly available today. From brain scanners, to fetal monitoring, to endoscopes, to lasers, to radioactive chemicals, all are computerized. Most hospitals use modern technology as assistance in the operating room. For example, some doctors use new machines to treat very complex illness, which effectively cures people and prolongs life expectancy around the world. There are a lot of people though, who still struggle with health concerns, and some people do not have access to a healthcare facility.

Modern technology has also created new diseases and discomforts, such as obesity, laziness and personality disorders. Exposure to digital signals and emissions from cell phone and microwaves has altered our moods, produced sleep irregularities, headaches, poor memory, mental excitement, confusion, anxiety, depression, appetite disturbance, and immune system problems.

There is another concern about our health and modern technology -- plastic surgery. We have advanced in this field. For example, silicone breast implants caused systematic disease, as well as autoimmune issues and varieties of other health concerns. Dow Corning, the manufacturer of medical silicon, was sued repeatedly in 1998, because of the damage caused by silicon, and drove the company into bankruptcy. People become dissatisfied with their looks; they want to change their nose, or the thickness of their lips. Modern technology can offer that to people, but in the long run people became disenchanted with the whole body.

This is why a great number of people today suffer from Body Dysmorphic Disorder. Modern technology has contributed to low self-image, because people tend to compare themselves to movie stars and never measure up to them, so they internalize a low self-concept. Modern technology has produced anxiety; people in general are anxious and apprehensive. Sometimes, people are clear about the source of their anxiety, but often, they have baseless anxiety, which is imagined. The mind of modern man is filled with fears and anxiety; 90% of the time, these fears and anxiety are irrational and untrue.

DDT, the modern pesticide, has been used for many years to reduce Malaria and Yellow fever, and to fight other mosquito-borne diseases, but it does great harm to vegetation. Other heath includes vaccinations and their relationship with autism. We know vaccinations are a modern miracle, which eliminated diseases that ravaged humanity, like polio, diphtheria, and smallpox. In 1990, accusations began to surface those children's vaccinations where responsible for the rise in the rate of autism in the population. Some parents refuse to inoculate their children. They think the body has an immune system that can fight every illness that may face us in our daily life. There are few countries around the world, however, which do not impose vaccinations on their children, and it seems they are winning the battle. All that shows us how much the advancement in modern technology can be helpful in most instances, but also can be harmful to us. It can produce new diseases, or augment old ones.

The psychological effects of modern technology. One part of the population impacted severely is the elderly, left at nursing homes making them feel isolated from their offspring. Their sons and daughters are busy with work and forget their parents, or do not have time for them, because they want to make a living in this brutal reality. Another psychological effect is when people start to dress the same, and lead the same lifestyle. We call it sameness. They build the same house, drive the same cars, and try to look like everybody else in the neighborhood. We have lost the uniqueness of our individuality. Moreover, the rapid advancement of technology has made our patience run thin. We want everything fast, because life is going fast. The prevailing attitude seems to be, "well everybody is doing it and I want to be part of the crowd, or part of the herd." The profound psychological effect modern technology introduced is <u>the herd mentality</u>. Be part of the crowd; do not try to be different, because that may harm the cohesiveness of the community. In a herd mentality, there is no place for creative individuality. It is easy for the herd to be led; thus, this idea is very appealing to dictators.

Thanks to modern technology, people are less interactive physically, or face to face. They lose their skills of connectedness. Life has become more complex but we hardly ever notice it, because technology has made complexity simpler than ever. From the beginning, mankind has engaged in the acquisition of things which he deems necessary to his physical, mental and emotional well-being. Some of these things are basic and essential to life itself, like food, water, clothing and shelter. Other things may not be necessary for the basic maintenance of life itself, but may add greatly to a person's quality of life.

Ironically, the more technological advancement we have, the more we feel isolated from one another. We substitute an electronic relationship for a physical one. Too much electronic connection gives us a sense of social isolation. Furthermore, emotional visibility cannot be seen through the Web. People have a penchant to say things in the electronic world which they would never say to people in person. The person with whom they are communicating is not physically present to display an emotional reaction when we are communicating electronically. It's as if the part of our nervous system that registers the feelings of others has been paralyzed or removed. As when we are drunk, we do not realize or do not care that our words are hurting others.

Modern man is not happy with what he has invented. We have all these sophisticated communication tools, but we have become distant from each other. We become shy and do not approach each other. Barriers are wider between people, even among family members. Loneliness, isolation, and poor connections are dominant today. As a result, people suffer from more anxiety, depression and social phobia.

Environmental pollution and modern technology. We are pumping 30 billion tons of CO_2 a greenhouse gas linked to global temperature increase, into our atmosphere each year. The effects of this problem are both long term and cumulative. Sadly many people do not realize the full extent of this problem. There is a total greenhouse emission of 33.376 million tons across the globe. Consider the level of deforestation in developed countries in the name of industrialization. The trash that is produced daily in the world, and put in a landfill, is compounding the problem because we are running out of space.

The most dangerous environmental damage is deforestation. The wealthier countries are cutting the trees of the poorer countries. It is the ultimate abuse, and the native people who depend on the forest for their survival are living below the poverty level. The forest is the lung of the planet and if we lose it, there will be unintended consequences. For example, the forests of Brazil and Indonesia are in very critical condition. Man is heartless when it comes to satisfying his insatiable desire for more and more comfort. The cruelty that has been committed toward our environment is beyond imagination, and we all are responsible to the next generation. What kind of legacy are we leaving? A legacy of greed, selfishness, and carelessness, all as a result of modern technology, which allows man to be more skillful in his abuse of his fellow humans.

Modern technology has damaged the environment severely, in all aspects. No doubt, the upcoming generation will suffer tremendously. The quality of the air is very poor; look at China and the quality of their air. It is toxic to the respiratory system. Is it worth it that China produces cheap toys, and in return pollutes its air? That is the ultimate stupidity. But human beings are irrational, and often seek their own destruction. People often look to immediate satisfaction, not considering long term damage. This myopic view has had a disastrous impact on our environment. We are at the point of no return; we cannot undo the damage.

Nuclear energy. Currently nuclear energy is one of the few forms of energy which can produce a vast amount of power in a relatively small area, and economically, without producing carbon dioxide waste. It is safe and fine until an accident takes place. The worst examples are the nuclear accident at Three Mile Island in New York, or in Chernobyl in the Soviet Union. Now, we are faced with nuclear pollution, and that affects our vegetation. If the land becomes poisonous, nothing will grow and radiation may last years and years.

The attitude of mankind toward nature. There is a tremendous effect of plastics on the earth, and effects of pesticides on our food. Overfishing has caused incredible damage and unbalanced the environment. Man, by his nature, is very selfish and greedy. Thus, he will not hesitate to abuse natural resources, whether in the sea, the earth, or the air. Man, with his shortsightedness, has acted irresponsibly and carelessly. Such attitudes have brought a painful reality about our environment. Undoubtedly future generations will curse us for our abusive attitudes to our beloved planet. Mankind is wasteful; we throw tons of food away every year, while our brothers in Africa are starving. Modern man has butchered animals to eat or for entertainment; even the enormous elephant is not safe from his knife. As Gandhi put it, "there is enough for everybody's needs, but not for human greed." The troubling reality is, do we really need all these materials just to satisfy our unnecessary greed. The consequences on our environment are unimaginable.

Modern technology and human abuse. Technology has made life more complex. Sweatshops and harsher forms of slavery are more likely to be found in technologically advanced societies, versus more primitive societies. More people are starving, in total numbers and per-capital, in the most technologically advanced age than at any other point in history. Since modern technology requires a level of intelligence for us to survive, there are some unfortunate people who do not have enough intelligence to navigate through life. Thus, they are abused by the rest of us, because in the core of man's heart is selfish and greedy, unless the power of compassion takes over. But that can be very far from reality, and it's a dream to think man has evolved to be a spiritual, rather than brutal, creature.

Modern technology and human inspiration. We need to be mindful that part of life is not materials. It's other things, such as unconditional love, hope, compassion, knowledge, understanding, and others, which come from a place not found within our hard drive. We need to know where the world is taking us, but at the same time, realize we cannot get swallowed up by the madness of technological advancement. We must constantly remind ourselves of what is really important in life. The world cannot lose its humanity, plain and simple. We must forever hold onto what truly makes us human. The brain, the soul, the spirit, the earth, the brotherhood, and human justice and beauty, make up the core values of connection.

What makes us real humans is when we take into consideration the well-being of our brothers and sisters on the planet, whether they live in the Congo or the Netherlands. As Khalil Gibran put it, "we all are fingers of one loving hand of God". As Einstein put it, "problems cannot be solved at the same level of awareness that created them." We need a different level of awareness to control the danger that is facing our survival as a result of massive technological advancement.

Chapter Fourteen

Military Spending = Foolish Spending

The whole army and navy are unproductive laborers;
they should serve the public.

-- Adam Smith, *The Wealth of Nations*

It is an insane world. We are arming ourselves to the teeth, under
the pretext of security. By arming ourselves we are creating a
more dangerous world. The armament industry tends to engender
fear in people and give them justification to have more arms.
The machine of propaganda plays with people's psychology. In
general, people are naïve and unsophisticated in their views,
and they believe such justification. Thus, security and worry
are inflated and exaggerated, and we often do not differentiate
between imagined or real security.

There are two types of assault on the human community as a
result of military spending. One is the assault on the environment.
Nuclear wastes are incredible, and have touched all the aspects of
life. The cancer rate is very high in areas with nuclear waste. The
second assault is on the psyche of people. People are suspicious
of others, with the world divided between us, and our enemies.
Almost every country in the world has created an enemy, whether
real or imagined.

The arms industry is driven by profit motive only; they are not concerned about anything other than profits. Again, that is the ugly side of human greed. They have created uncertainty, and made armament the norm, not the exception. We seek more advanced weaponry so we can make others tremble in fear. The arms industry represents a perpetual cash-cow, and we milk it endlessly. Humans need new lenses to see through the deception of the arms industry.

We need to redirect the colossal financial resources that are currently spent on the military to education, housing, building roads, building hospitals, feeding the malnourished, a good retirement for the elderly and promoting creativity. Military expenditures consistently impede economic development. The highest levels of military spending are in both less developed and developed countries, which prevents them from fulfilling the basic economic and social rights of their people. That can be a serious impediment to the economic growth.

What the wise men think of war. Every gun that is made, every warship launched, and every rocket fired signifies a theft from those who hungry and are not fed, cold and are not clothed. Every penny spent in arms is not just money alone; it is spending the sweat of laborers, the genius of scientists, and the hopes of children. This is not a way of life at all in any true sense. Under the cloud of war, it is humanity hanging on a cross of iron (Dwight D. Eisenhower). Nations that continue year after year to spend more money on military defense than on social programs are approaching spiritual doom. (Dr. Martin Luther King, Jr.).

"When l was in the military, they gave me a medal for killing two men, and discharged me for loving one" (Leonard Matlovich). This brings me to the worst aspect of our hard life: the military system, which l abhor. This black spot on civilization ought to be abolished with all possible speed. "Heroism on command, senseless violence, and all the loathsome nonsense that goes by the name of patriotism, how passionately l hates them" (Albert Einstein).

In arming, we create a more dangerous world. That is simple logic. When we arm ourselves that in itself creates fear within other people, who in return arm themselves. All countries of the planet are arming themselves, and conflict will be inevitable. Since every country is arming itself, they believe they have the large penis to attack. It is always about the penis; that is the psychoanalytic interpretation of armament. Each nation is trying to show the other that they have the larger penis. It is a clear representation of fear within us, and we try to assuage that fear.

The psychological dynamic of the armaments. If we talk about arming countries, normally that is done by man. Often, man has a serious fear of castration, according to Freud. In the early years of a man's life, the fear of castration comes from women, but when he becomes an adult that fear can also come from others. A whole country can become fearful of being castrated by another country. Having a large penis, in the form of arms, gives the whole country some sense of security and some temporary relief from anxiety and fear.

Another psychological explanation of war and armaments has to do with menstruation. Men do not menstruate on a monthly basis, but women see the blood all their lives. Man does not see the blood. Thus, he develops menstruation envy; he wants to see blood. Therefore, he wages a war. However, women abhor war. Because of her constant bleeding on a monthly basis, and she is fed up with seeing blood. Some tribes in Africa have realized this hidden and unconscious desire within man, and came up with a practice to give men some relief. They make a cut in the penis when a man reaches puberty and make him bleed for few days, so he can see his similarity to the girls in the tribe when they reach puberty. That can reduce his desire for blood. Consequently, it reduces his desire to fight and shed blood. It would be fascinating if there is a follow up study of those men, to see if they are the same as other men, or if their desire to fight and be aggressive is less.

There are two motives that push man to continue to build more and more sophisticated arms. The first, stronger motive is sexuality, and the second motive is aggression. Military spending is part of aggression, to find a means to destroy others. We come up with ridiculous justifications for arming ourselves. We dehumanize our supposed enemy. Even if we do not have a real enemy, we have to create one. That can give us justification and frees us from guilt.

Man is going to wake up one of these days, and realize he has destroyed the planet with enormous military spending. We are also causing huge damage to the environment, almost to the point of no return. Our environment is suffering from chemical arms, and the experiments conducted by the military on people or on animals have dire consequences. For example, most wars have left mines underground, and great numbers of people in Cambodia are losing their legs. Chemical gas used in wars has affected the earth severely, and the damage is so permanent that for more than two hundred years those areas cannot grow any kind of vegetation. That is exactly what happened in northern Iraq, when Saddam used chemical gas on the Kurds, and killed more than five thousand people. The survivors had to leave the land because they cannot grow anything there. Spending money on armaments is the most stupid and idiotic action man ever performed.

As far as security, the world is becoming a more dangerous place to be. Imagine for a moment (as in the John Lennon song, *Imagine*) that we live in a world without guns, tanks, warplanes, or naval ships. Undoubtedly, it would be a safer place than our present world. But conflict is inevitable, and it erupts almost monthly, and often we have to settle it with arms.

To summarize, the motive for military spending is propaganda which has no basis in rational thinking. Man fears his fellow man, and that pushes him to create the military machine. Fear of each other is almost embedded in the fabric of our unconscious mind. That comes through the generations, since Cane killed his brother Abel. Thus we inherited fear and a mistrust of others. The pretext of security is just a myth, because the more arms we have, the more insecure we become. Hence, more arms constitute serious threats to our neighbors. In response they will arm themselves thus launching an arms race. Each one wants to out-do the other until we reach a state of no return, when we can destroy ourselves with the push of a button. It is an insane world in which we live.

We build up arms, because we do not see ourselves as brothers and sisters. Instead, we see each other as foes, and when we build such technology, soon it will become obsolete. Because of the rapid advancement of technology, we have to develop more, and then we are in an arms race. That makes the world unsafe, and we do not wish our children to live in such an unpredictable and cruel world.

If we come back to our genuine sense of compassion and save the money we spend on arms, we will see a world free from poverty and disease, with fresh clean water for every single citizen on the planet, with medical care that suits everyone. The human community would live in a wonderful world. The money spent in arms in every country is beyond our imagination, and very hard to calculate. The wonderful world scenario above is just a dream, and man cannot or will not make it possible, because of his innate nature of aggression and the desire to be better than his neighbor, or even control his neighbor.

Chapter Fifteen

The Measles of Mankind -- Nationality

Einstein said incredible wisdom, and it should be written in gold and put on the paper currency of every country: "Nationalism is an infantile disease; it is the measles of mankind." Nationality denotes a strong association of individuals and groups with a national identity, in the interest of a nation. Nationalism, on the other hand, is like cheap alcohol. First, it makes you drunk, then it makes you blind, then it kills you, or you kill yourself for the sake of your country. Nationalism is our form of incest; it is idolatry; it is our insanity. Nationality intolerance can be as bitter and unfair as religious intolerance has ever been, and it possesses a peculiar vulgarity of its own. The self-laudation of a people is more grotesque, because it is more self-centered, than the fanaticism of any creed.

Chauvinism. There is another form of human idiotic thought: people who inhabit a certain land feel they are better than other people, or even better than their neighbor. This is a part of psychological dysfunction; we have to differentiate ourselves from other people, so we can see ourselves as special and the rest as mediocre. It's as if God created different classes of people. Some of them are cheap and some are expensive. In reality, what we do is turn human beings into commodities. Mankind is struggling within, due to his aggressive motive. In the bottom of his soul he has not matured yet. Thus he engages in wars and discrimination. That gives his restless soul some soothing comfort. But, he may create more problems for himself, because of his chauvinistic attitudes which will be faced with rejection and hostility from others. And that puts him in a cycle of rejection and hostility. Thus, from the expulsion of Adam and Eve from the Garden of Eden until today, we have engaged in endless wars and conflicts that cost humanity inordinate amounts of pain and suffering.

Whether we like it or not, that is part of the satisfaction of our aggressive tendencies, although, because aggression is built in our human psyche, we may not live in peace at all. God sent many of prophets and messengers, and His instructions were very clear: I created you with an aggressive tendency, but I want you to cultivate your unselfish nature and non-aggressive tendency. Unfortunately, it seems the biology of man overrode the message of God and the manifested in the beginning of the universe, when God advised Adam and Eve not to eat the pomegranate, but they disregarded the order of God and followed their corrupt tendency. This is why we have created nationality and surrounded ourselves with borders so no one can get in; when you do not allow people to get in, you make yourself special and you look down at people from other nationalities. That is what we see today; the system of passports and visas are a manifestation of putting up barriers to not let people in, so you can have the sense of importance.

The symbol. We have created a flag, and people die for that flag. That is the creation of a simple mind, and what a dumb thing to do. We selected cheap cloths of different colors and assigned incredible value to it. People bow to the flag, because this piece of cloth is secret, and people rally around it. Human beings are superstitious; they assigned magical power to nonliving things. (Remember, we used to worship idols made of stone.) Human beings are fabulous idiots as far as making the love of land or flag a moral or a virtue; it is ludicrous.

Nationality appeals to man's blindness, to his power of self-sacrifices and to the petty arrogance that makes the individual value only himself and those who immediately resemble him. We are the only chosen people; that have been heard from many people in one form or another. And it has been the battle cry of every nation bent on conquest.

There is nothing in the entire world worth fighting for. We need to understand that a true nation exists for the common good of everybody. No empires can be held together merely by force. That is a stupid thing, because that we think there is no one nation that can exhaust the infinite varied possibilities of humanity. Foolish poverty is the belief that many nationalities have it all. It is stupid to believe one man could sum up all men. The divinity of mankind, however, has been drenched with blood and horror, because of nationality.

We need to help the individual to have sufficient fairness of mind to consider others beside himself. Immanuel Kant laid down the rule that every man must be treated as an end in himself, never merely as a means. Furthermore, Goethe insisted that mankind could only be made by all men, just as the world was only made by many. Goethe talked about the power of the spirit. No man is right, he said, unless he heals the striving spirits, and understands others, although he should be understood as well.

The values of diversity and self-preservation. Diversity -- different people from different backgrounds, different skin colors and different national origins can live together in harmony -- gives any country incredible power, because in variety we truly see the beauty of the universe. Imagine that you live in a place where people are all the same. They eat the same food, dress the same, join the same organization and celebrate the same holidays. What a boring life, to live among those people! The beauty in life is to live a colorful one, whether in the way we dress, the way we eat our food, or the way we manage our life. As far as self-preservation, we may preserve ourselves by being open to a different culture. Let us take a wonderful example, the United State of America. It is the strongest nation in the world, because the country preserves itself by having diverse citizens who came from all parts of the world. People preserve themselves by being helpful to each other. If they do not do that, they will not survive or flourish. Thus, diversity and cooperation can sustain any society. Isolation, in which nations close themselves off from the rest of the world, will definitely cause them to perish.

The concept of patriotism. Another form of nationality is patriotism, which means you put your own nation above humanity, above the principle of justice and truth. The love for one country which is not part of one's love for humanity, is not love, it is idolatrous worshiping. A love for one individual which excludes the love for another is not love. As George Bernard Shaw said, "patriotism is your conviction that this country is superior to all others because you were born in it." George Orwell also indicated that nationalism is about power, and acquiring as much power and prestige as possible for the nation in which a man submerges his individuality. Thus nationalism, accordingly to this concept, is a form of aggression.

Patriotism is defensive. It is devotion to a particular place and the way of life one thinks best, but has no wish to impose on others. Leo Tolstoy, the Russian novelist and thinker judged patriotism harshest among all. He sees it as stupid and immoral. According to him, it is stupid because every country holds themselves to be the best. Obviously, since only one country can be qualified, it is immoral because it enjoins us to promote our country's interest at the expense of all other countries and by any means, including war. That is at odds with the most basic rule of morality, which tells us not to do to others what we would not want them to do us. American politician George Kateb argues that patriotism is a mistake twice over. It is typically a grave moral error and its source is typically a state of mental confusion.

Patriotism is most importantly expressed in a readiness to die and kill for one's country. But a country is not a discernible individual; it is rather an abstract thing, a compound of a few actual and many imaginary ingredients. History falsely sanitized or falsely considered heroism as a sense of kinship to a largely invented purity, and of social ties that are largely invisible or impersonal.

Define patriotism as a special concern for one's country's well-being, that is not exclusive and having aggressive concern for it. This type of patriotism is irrational, and morally hazardous. While Viroli indicated totally different views of the patriot, he said we have a moral obligation toward our country, because we are indebted to it. We owe our country our life, our education, our language, and in the most fortunate case, our liberty. We have received these things at least in part, by serving the country's good. He was echoing Socrates' views. Both Socrates and Viroli are exaggerating the benefits bestowed on us by our country; surely any gratitude owed for being born or brought up is owed to our parents, rather than a nation.

We can think of patriots as an aggregate of individuals; do we owe them a debt of gratitude for the benefits of life among them? We need to look to the issue of political obligation to the country we live in, which is to obey the law and act as a citizen. We also need to look to the universal duties toward our fellow man, not just on the particular real estate we occupy. Mason indicated citizenship has intrinsic value, because the virtue of being a citizen is being a member of a collective body in which all enjoy equal status and are thereby provided with recognition.

Why do people love their country? Or, why they are loyal to it? Patriotism involves endorsement of one's country. Loyalty is virtue and goes without questioning. We think of patriotism as a natural and appropriate expression of attachment to the country in which we were born and raised, and gratitude for the benefits of life on its soil, among its people, and under its laws. Some may argue that patriotism is morally mandatory, or even the core of morality. Loyalty or attachments are a type of group egoism, and it can be at odds with the demands of universal justice, and common human solidarity. Love of one's own country characteristically goes together with dislike and hostility toward other countries. Such an attitude may encourage militarism and create international tension and conflict, although now, there is a sweeping cosmopolitanism that allows for no attachment or loyalty to one's country and compatriots.

Patriotism and humanity. Melian Stawell in his article in the *International Journal of Ethics*, indicated it is patriotism for which almost all the nations are at each other's throats. It caused, or helped to cause, this appalling tragedy, this welter of courage and fury, at once so horrible, so sublime, and so foolish. All over the world, millions of men and women are ready to give up their lives for their countries. At least it is not for lack of raw spiritual force that the world must undergo such unfathomable misery; it seems that there is some comfort in such darkness. There is enough heroism on the planet to make a heaven right here on earth, if we could only unite the wills of nations instead of each defying the other to the death! There is a grim doctrine that the sole duty of any ordinary citizen is duty to his country, for the sake of power and domination. Jingoism is another extreme form of nationalism in which the individual who lives in a particular country sees that his country is superior to all other countries. That itself can cause conflict for the rest of us, while the healthy perspective of another nation's citizens ought to be as sacred as our own. It is common sense, of common humanity.

But unfortunately, we have a natural bias, a defective education system, and narrow statesmanship, and that can erect barriers. If we add to it the differences of traditions outlooks on life, life with each other can be impossible. The fact is, a nation cannot live alone. It is the give and take that allows us to survive.

The figment of our imagination. Why are patriots loyal to their country? What is so good about it? The patriot is an endorsement of the country, and adherence to patriotism tends to be a type of group egotism, meaning morally arbitrary partiality to 'one's own' and lack of doubt is at odds with the demands of universal justice and common human solidarity. The love of one's country goes hand in hand with hostility toward other countries. It tends to encourage militarism, and makes for international tension and conflict.

Machiavelli in the 1500s said the paramount interest of one's country overrides any moral consideration with which they might come into conflict. To do the job well, there are promises to deceive, dissemble and use violence, sometimes in cruel ways and on a large scale, when political circumstances require such actions. The mature individual citizen becomes a moral agent, and has in his heart the best interests of mankind, not merely his own self-interest.

Colonization. There is unbridled lust for power in itself, regardless of any further end. The temptations that cluster around this desire are perhaps the deepest in man. People certainly desire power much more than the desire for money. In fact, usually they only want money for the sake of power. Goethe saw that the fundamental cause of war is the ghost of man, desiring more power over his fellow man. Man wins the power by force and by force keeps his hold; he cannot rule his own unruly heart. In colonization, normally the citizens hold the desire for comfort, love of life, and hope for domination. It also brings the gain of territory, which is the gain of power. Here the conqueror can dictate his will on people and obey his thirst for domination and control.

Colonization is the intoxication with over-estimation of ourselves, which makes us all confuse our own selfishness with the divine task to civilize the world. War increases the power of a nation and deludes its citizens with a vain-glorious and idolatrous worship of their own civilization. They dream of it as universal superiority, but will not see all the horror along the way to that goal. Always, colonization associates with wars, because there is no nation that would allow itself to be colonized. Thus, war spreads fear, and consequently we nurse the spirit of revenge. Imagine the cycle we wind up in. As humans, we want to nurse the egos of each other, since our ego is like a pampered child who wants to be the center of attention. Thus, we became so sophisticated that we invented the concept of nationality, so that collectively we can nurse each other's ego, and support the pathology of being better than others.

When God created the universe. People have inhabited earth, and they have multiplied in different races. They roam the earth without any problems. Until the world population increased astronomically, then we started to become territorial, which springs out of our self-centeredness, or limited resources, or the sophistication of man to control his fellow humans? Humanity has been through five eras: hunting, gathering, agriculture, industrial, and presently we live in the information age. Throughout the first four eras, we moved very freely with no boundaries. With the arrival of the information age, we started to keep records of everything; we issued passports and visas, and marked boundaries. Then we started to fight among ourselves over land, and that was when the concept of nationality emerged (about 200 years ago), and the "measles" started to infect us.

The accident of birth. Please follow me with this logic: You happened to be born in Brazil, or Sweden, or Japan. But why on the earth do you feel proud of the place of your birth, when you had no say over it? You did not choose the place you born, whether Japan or Mongolia. You were born as the result of the pleasure of two people. Often, our parents do not even love each other. If it just happened to be that your mother and father met in Mongolia, and you came to be as a result, why do you feel proud to be from a place when you had no choice in the matter? You may be lucky if you were born in Europe, and not lucky to be born in Somalia. But attachment to the land on which you were born is something absurd and foolish, and even more foolish and ludicrous when we engage in a war to defend that land. Who has the land? Nobody truly owns the land. And, what makes this country or that country holier than any other country? This is the invention of our selfish mind.

When Almighty God expelled us from heaven, He never said to his messengers, that is the land for Canadians, and this is the land for Indians. But the human aggressive tendency pushed us to divide the land and establish borders, and now you must also have a passport to get in. We like to complicate our lives, and we like to put barriers among us. Barriers make us feel better, and as far as complicating lives, this is what they are for. We do not like to facilitate, or make our lives simple. We like to put hindrances in front of ourselves and others, and the more hindrances that l put in your way, the better l feel about me. That gives some satisfaction to my sadistic tendency, of which we all have some elements, unless you realize it, and put a cap on the evil part of your self.

Since we know this is absurd, why do we do it anyway? It is the sense of belonging to a certain group of people, and one has to differentiate himself. Since people came up with idea of nationality, it works, in most instances, to nurture our collective ego. That gives me a false sense of meaning, but in reality it is an engagement in mass pathology. Nationality is a disease and once we participate in such a disease, we are internalizing some of societal pathology and dysfunction. Sadly, this is exactly the human condition right now. How can we free ourselves from the pathology of nationality? It requires a collective consciousness and shifting of our paradigm of understanding, to look at everyone as brothers and sisters. This perhaps is a remote dream; humanity is not mature enough to be at such a level. So why do I write about it? Sincerely, l just wants to bring it to the level of awareness of people. Perhaps, one of these days, people may realize what kind of mess that they have put themselves in, and try to use logic and gain the sense of brotherhood.

Critical thinking is the answer. The paradigm of patriotism has been established collectively, through subtle conditioning throughout human history. To face that, we have to introduce critical thinking within the thought processes of ourselves and others. As Plato said "an unexamined life is not worth living." For example, patriotism for some people is virtue, while for others it converges with religious faith, predicated on the assumption that their nation enjoys special status in the eyes of God.

The problem of pride, patriotism, racism, and saluting flags, is that it fosters that it's fashionable to degrade your neighbors. It is the herd mentality; we put people into groups and tally their differences and weaknesses, rather than their wonderful qualities. Psychologically speaking, humans love to categorize each other. Thus, racism was born. People cling to a flag, or worship the ground they stand upon as if it were sacred earth, while we have no trouble filling that land we love with our waste, and polluting it with the byproducts of industry and capital. People pledge allegiance to the soil and flag. As Dr. Johnson said, "patriotism is the last refuge of the scoundrel." We have to do some soul-searching, identify our distorted thinking and transform ourselves, evolving to the level of human decency. At that level, we will take into consideration the well-being of our neighbor, not just act according to our own selfish reasons.

To sum up, nationality is one of the destructive behaviors that we perpetuate. The consequences are enormous, such as division, separation, hostility, military spending, wars, conflict, and most of all, the drainage of our collective energy. The power of compassion can unify us and make the world a hospitable place for all, because in the end we all are fingers of one loving hand, which is the hand of God.

Chapter Sixteen

Spiritual Pollution

We are all hurt by environmental pollution, but have we thought about spiritual pollution? First of all, we may need to define pollution. Webster's Dictionary defines pollution as: impure, dirty, making things unclean, corrupt, contaminated, filthy, and desecrated. We are living in a polluted world because we are greedy and want to get everything fast and easy, without an ounce of care about the earth.

We dumped everything into our rivers, lakes, seas and on the land. We built factories all over the world, without looking at ways we could protect our environment. Now, however, we are becoming aware of the damage we caused to the environment, and there are some movements working today to teach us to pay more attention to our environment. We are getting sick more than ever, and pollution is becoming seriously toxic to our health and well-being.

In this chapter, however, I am addressing spiritual pollution, which can be more dangerous than environmental pollution. The primary contributor to spiritual pollution is war and the killing of people. When there are killings in a certain place, that place becomes polluted, and dark energy tends to cover up the place. Consequently, the living conditions of people there become difficult and can be nerve-racking. When a person is killed, the energy of the body and the spirit may stay attached to that place for a while.

Thus, many killings in one place can attract more killing, and pollute the entire area. Killing attracts killing. That is what has happened in Palestine, Syria, Afghanistan, Iraq, and parts of Africa. Those places are infused with a huge amount of human blood, and that is a magnet for more killing. As a result, the evil forces take over. Since energy of the spirit cannot be killed, only the physical part of the body, the energy does not leave a particular place. So, killing human beings can have the utmost detrimental effect upon the psychological climate of a location, and it may last for several years, or even decades.

Hence, we need to cleanse these places of spiritual pollution, through establishing a civil society based on respect for the sanctity of life. For example, European countries have been in horrible wars, but have now stopped killing, and are building a society based on the acceptance of others' differences. What is needed in Afghanistan, Syria, Iraq, and Palestine is a cessation of the killing and the commencement of a major cleaning of souls by accommodating the different views among their populations.

Another part of spiritual pollution is the negative energy that people carry. For example, if a person is depressed, and molecules of his breath are in the air, everyone can breathe it in and they will get infected, just like the transmission of other infections. Soon, we all suffer from a blue mood, depression, anxiety, phobias, aggression, or envy, and engage in negative talk about others.

All these are contributors to the production of spiritual pollution. It can affect any person without ever being aware of it. For example, have you been in a place and felt nervous and wanted to leave right away? I am sure you have. That place had an accumulation of negative energy, because thoughts, words, and actions have energy that remains there. That is why one needs to be very careful about the process of one's thinking; your actions and behavior can have a profound impact on others as well as on you, yourself.

Spiritual pollution can also be the result of interactions with an individual's surroundings. For example, if we live in a crowded area, the chance of having trouble is greater than if we live in an open space. Cement buildings are very unhealthy for us; wood is better because wood is closer to nature. It is not synthetic, and synthetic things can have negative interactions upon us. For example, modern cities across the world are not healthy places to live because developers poured a lot of cement with little attention to planting trees. That is why crime can flourish in a big, crowded city, while living in the countryside can be more relaxing.

Spiritual pollution is contagious. We are all one human community, whether we live in Brazil or in India, so if something happens to a person in Brazil, a person in India can be affected. For example, if a person is suffering from flu, the air can transfer the illness to other parts of the world. Thus, the physical health of people around the world is a matter that concerns all of us, because we all share this small planet earth, and if someone has something harmful, it can transfer to another person in a different part of the world. No one is immune from such interaction. We do not live in isolation. Even the person who lives in a remote village in Egypt can be hurt by the depression of a person in Cuba.

Spiritual pollution is difficult to clean up, because it requires many generations to follow the path of peace and positive energy. While we can use modern technology to clean up environmental pollution, how do we clean up spiritual pollution? For example Afghanistan is a place with no natural resources. It is a barren land of mountains and rocks, and has been a magnet for spiritual pollution as a result of wars, and the loss of many lives. That attracts more and more killing. How do we clean it up? The first step is for people to stop hurting each other. That may require a different level of awareness than what they currently have. As Albert Einstein said, "Problems cannot be solved at the same level of awareness that created them." We need a different level of awareness and understanding, the awareness that human life is worthwhile. If a person carries a different opinion than mine, it does not mean that I have to eliminate him. But, this is exactly what is happening in Afghanistan, Iraq, and Syria. People do not tolerate differences there.

What might be the solution? The educational system might play a crucial role in helping people realize that differences can be very healthy for human growth, and much better than using them as a reason to end the life of others. The key to cleaning up spiritual pollution is education, but what kind of education? It is the type of education and awareness that makes people transcends the dark side of their souls and accepts others as partners with whom to share the earth.

Conclusion. Spiritual pollution can be a breeding ground for evil forces to prevail. Spiritual pollution hurts all of us, not just those in the place where it grows. This is why it is imperative that all of us get involved and correct the trend of violence currently in several places around world. We also need to instill a sense of compassion in our children, so that when they grow up, they do not participate in spiritual pollution.

Our journey is limited to a certain number of years on planet earth. Thus, our responsibility is to live in peace within ourselves, as well as with others. Of course, that is easier said than done. So, what do we do? As Albert Einstein indicated, we need to create and foster a high level of awareness among people in general, to appreciate each other and conceal the ugly face of humanity. We need to evolve spiritually and try to clean our hearts and souls of malice and hatred. As Buddha said, "do not kill your enemy; kill the hate in your heart toward him, so you can be a free and highly evolved human being.

Chapter Seventeen

The Swan vs. Ugly Duckling Syndrome:

The Psychology of Beauty and Ugliness

We are recognized and we derive our identity from the surface of our body. A less attractive body is not a sealed unit, but ugliness is unknown inside the body. We view our body as a vulnerable construction of flesh, blood, skin and organs. Or maybe we view our body as a bag of meat that carry our soul to the final destination.

Sadly, we have put too much of a premium on the body. Instead of living comfortably inside our bodies, it has become a burdensome. We entertain all kinds of illness, and our bodies become a theater in which we act out our pathology or neurosis. Remember, whatever we plant in our mind, we tend to harvest in our body.

Primitive woman did not have plastic surgery to correct her nose, or spend trillions of dollars in cosmetic products, just to mask imagined flows, and to presumably beautify her body.

The premium perception on our body is particularly true with women; it is almost to the point that her body becomes the measurement for her acceptance of herself and of success in life. Men have different standards to relate to the world, such as accomplishments or achievements, to measure acceptance and success. Normally we value women through their attractiveness and physical beauty, while we value men through their accomplishments. This assessment of women has cost us trillions and trillions of dollars as a society, just to satisfy a woman's hunger to appear beautiful and charming.

We all love to look at a beautiful woman; we talk about her, wonder about her. She gets it all: the great job, beautiful friends, men falling over themselves to be noticed by her, and doors being opened for her, both literally and figuratively. Let's face it, when we meet someone new, a first impression is formed from looks. Only later do things such as personality, intelligence and character start to take on meaning. (A side note about beauty: weight is not much of a factor, unless the person is morbidly obese or skinny to the point of being anorexic.) The key to perceived beauty is the face. Daniel Hamermesh, in his book *Beauty Pays*, found that beauty is absolutely connected with success, at least financial success.

The Princess Syndrome. Companies that place a premium on hiring attractive people have an average higher revenue then similar companies, which do not. Often, beautiful women get away with things ordinary people cannot. A beautiful woman can form a bigger-than-life persona, working at a higher level than normal self-esteem. Couple that with the feeling she is "special" and deserves the best, it becomes a self-fulfilling prophecy. Thus, a beautiful woman may not pay attention to her personal or intellectual development. She may rely on her physical beauty to carry her through. She may develop histrionic characteristics so she can be the center of attention and adoration, which is exactly what she wants. That may lead to depression, because if she does not receive enough adoration and compliments she will be depressed and angry.

The downside of beauty. A paradox: low self-esteem is more common in beautiful women than you may expect. Some just do not believe they are attractive, and have a distorted self-image. Some of them may say they have no talents, intelligence, or redeeming qualities, other than looks. Some are shy, withdrawn and most of society encourages them to be selfish. A beautiful woman is often an outcast, or makes another woman feel threatened or jealous, and, of course, the number one threat is her beauty. That threat may manifest when these women steal another's husband. Also, some men are intimidated by a beautiful woman.

As with most things, beauty can be a blessing, but it can also be a curse. As Penelope said, "I am intrigued by the way in which physical appearances can often direct a person's life." Things happen differently for beautiful women than for plain ones; different yes, but not necessarily better. The pretty woman may feel prettier around less attractive people and uglier around pretty people; this is automatic thinking. Unfortunately, our perceptions of things can be unconscious, and we tend to go along with that perception without a shred of doubt. It is almost ingrained in us. The literature in this area suggests less attractive people perhaps are nicer. Gorgeous people with supermodel faces are inevitability evil, poisonous, hags, while plain folks are funny, clever, charming and with saint-like behavior of Mother Teresa.

A woman's special beauty is not innate; it takes a lot of effort to maintain. The effort to control the body is evidenced by the proliferation of the weight control culture, cosmetic surgery and the cosmetics industry. Interestingly enough, a plastic surgeon in LA says that a nose job is so ubiquitous that it's becoming a gift for birthdays or Christmas. The beauty ideology forces women to subscribe to the culture of being feminine and fragile, and they are locked into their appearance as defining their values and worth.

Society in general tends to idealize attractive people. We put women on a pedestal, including those who do not earn it. However, research in this area shows beautiful people strive for conformity rather than independence, and for self-promotion rather than tolerance (Lihi Segal-Caspi). Normally we stereotype good-looking people with positive traits, but their traits may not good, but rather, bad ones. Moreover, women are their own worst critics when it comes to beauty; since they use beauty as a source of confidence, sometimes they may be more beautiful than they perceive themselves. As Eric Fromm said, "the most beautiful as well as the ugliest inclinations of man are not part of a fixed biologically given human nature, but result from the social process which creates man."

The other down side of beauty is that beautiful women tend to be narcissistic. Moreover, we are creating a culture for women who live inside of themselves and want the world to cater to their needs. Even when they get married and have children, they tend to make the world dance around them. This is why the divorce rate is higher among attractive women.

The reflection in the mirror. Inner beauty is important, but not nearly as important as outer beauty; beauty trumps goodness. Our internal mirror is often shaped by our parents, who give us a positive message that we are cute, and we tend to behave accordingly. Kids who are attractive face their own set of problems; they tend to be insecure as adults, especially if they are praised solely for their appearance. They may develop a harsh viewpoint for assessing of themselves.

The psychology of ugliness. Throughout history, ugliness has been associated with a whole series of negative terms such as imperfection, insignificance, failure, or even non-existence. Ugliness is the opposite of beauty, or the absence of beauty. Or, it can be defined as the failure of beauty. However, the measurement of ugliness and beauty can also be defined by the culture. For example, the culture of the Maasai tribes in Kenya sees the large ear lobe as a sign of beauty, while other cultures may see it a sign of ugliness. The small feet of Chinese women can be attractive to the Chinese, but in other cultures that can be considered unattractive; it's seen as the foot of a child. Therefore, ugliness and beauty are a reflection of cultural perceptions, and there is no standard of measurement that may be used for every culture. The island of Kiribati in the South Pacific considers morbid obesity the ultimate sign of beauty, while another culture could see the "toothpick" body frame as the ultimate beauty.

Operational definition of ugliness. The word ugly has been used meaning fearful, terrifying and hateful. A person with a deformity or a mutilated body part is often seen as frightening to others; ugliness induces anxiety. For many centuries being less attractive was linked with sin, greed, lewdness and decay, but a person can experience renewed wholeness and power through creative, reparative beauty.

Studies prove that less attractive people work harder at relationships, and at life in general. Thus, they tend to develop more character. Attractive people get more attention, so they do not work hard to improve their personality, and they do not develop character. This is why in American culture, blondes are said to be dumb...the "dumb blonde".

Less attractive people think from their heart, and tend to be compassionate. Attractive people are unfortunate; they attract negative energy to themselves, by being the center of attention and that makes them vulnerable to envious energy, which can bring them misfortune. That is exactly what is happening to fashion models around the world. Ugliness results from the emergence into consciousness of certain fantasies which alter a person's aesthetic sense in such a way that the formal qualities of experiences, shape, texture, and color become the sources of disturbance and the repulsive feeling. George R.R. Martin said, "is there any creature on earth as unfortunate as an ugly woman?"

Body Dysmorphic Disorder. It is a type of chronic mental illness is common mostly in women, because women cannot stop thinking about flaws in their appearance; flaws that are either minor or imagined. They feel their appearance is so shameful that they do not want to be seen by anyone. There is an intense obsession with appearance and body image. This perceived flaw causes them significant distress, and this obsession impacts their function in daily life. They seek numerous cosmetic procedures to fix perceived flaws, and even then are never satisfied. There is also a fear of having a deformity.

A woman can have a strong belief that she has an abnormal defect in her appearance, which causes her to stay home, or wear excessive makeup, even refuse to go out of the house. Women with this disorder tend to have some psychological or mental problems. For the obsession over perceived flaws, the course of treatment can be very difficult.

Current times can play a major role in developing psychological disturbances, because there is tremendous focus and pressure on appearance; there is a competition among people. This is why we spend trillions of dollars on cosmetics. This kind of disorder was not found in ancient cultures, because people did not focus on looks. Even today, it doesn't exist in primitive tribes, or remote cultures. Our modern culture puts incredible pressure on women to focus on their looks and ignore the essence of their being.

The social construction of gender. Appearance is one of the technologies of gender. The patriarchal regime of women defines and judges them through a fantasy model of beauty. As a result, the physical self becomes the core of women's self-conception, and there is a close relationship between physical attractiveness and the self–concept, to the extent that we value women through appearance only. Thus, the woman is placed in a no–win situation. She is expected to embody a timeless culture fantasy, and that removes her from the real essence of herself.

In today's society, the media stereotype of women has resulted in a perception of beauty that is often unattainable. Women compare themselves to an idealized standard of beauty, such as a fashion model. Richard Robins, Professor at the University of California-Davis, noted that when both men and women evaluate their intelligence, they do not compare themselves to Einstein, but rather to a more mundane standard, while women tend to compare themselves to supermodels. That can result in all manner of neuroses, such as eating disorders, or a poor self-image. There is an assumption in our society that beauty is an asset and ugliness a stigma.

The Platonic view. Beauty is love, or more accurately, desire, which extends from an animal's instinct to procreate. Freud said happiness in life is predominately sought through enjoyment of beauty. However, our new standard of measurement, in which men are supposed to be effective and women are supposed to be attractive, can be cumbersome on both. Because each one of us is trying to prove ourselves, women want to be a Barbie doll, and a man needs to be a super achiever. Such perceptions can box people into a role they are unable to fulfill.

The dualities of our lives. Our lives are based on either/or, good/evil, white/black, beautiful/ugly, right/wrong, happy/sad. We could, instead, look at life as it is, just to see it in front of us without labeling or judgment.

The humanistic view sees humans as light, and all radiate pleasing looks, because the focus here is not on the shell but on what is inside the shell. The body carries the soul and normally, the soul is beautiful because it comes from God, unless we pollute it with our wicked tendency. We are the center light of this world and God created everything for our service; in other words the whole world caters to us.

Finally, ultimately, good looks are not just a question of lucky birth. Physical appearance is evaluated alongside our body language, voice, and temperament. Charm can trump beauty; emotional expression and social skills are more important than beauty. If you are comfortable in your own skin, you become more appealing to others. Thus, you may spend less time at the mirror and more time engaging with the world. Beauty may be in the eye of the beholder, but attractiveness -- or the lack of it -- is culturally specific. The norm is culturally defined, like the faces of the tribes of Papua New Guinea.

Evolution Psychology. This branch of psychology has been given us a wonderful understanding of why we focus on looks. Poor looks mean poor genetic quality, and this is why less attractive women are reviled in almost every culture. Dr. Philippe Rushton's research indicates the survival of the "hottest", and he went further in his research to explain why the feminine movement has taken over, resulting in the feminization of Western society. Natural selection does not care about hurting feelings; all natural selection cares about is getting the best genes possible for each organism on which it acts. Beautiful people live easier lives, from nurses who give more attention to the pretty baby, to the school teacher who is more likely to blame less attractive students for trouble in the classroom. Beauty often can result in bigger paychecks, and beauty infers a healthy, strong immune system. Markus Rantala, a Finnish researcher, determined that a strong immune system can withstand high testosterone levels, and there is strong relationship between this stress hormone and infertility.

The astronomical waste of beauty products. It is bothersome how women purchase commodities for their bodies; they slather on cosmetics, change their hair color, have breast augmentation surgery, inject Botox into their face, and the list goes on and on. Men are told we should not objectify women, but a woman clearly engage in sexual objectification of their own bodies. How can we honor honesty, when a woman with a fake body is not being honest about herself? When women use cosmetics or have cosmetic surgery, they are committing fraud. There is a certain amount of deception and superficiality, and that can put our whole society on the deception loop.

The wasteful spending in cosmetic products works against evolution, because woman is not natural; in general, a man wants to see a woman the way she is, naturally. His concern is whether she is able to bear a healthy baby for him, and can withstand the test of time. Our modern world has invented millions of products just to cater to women's appearance. These products do not necessarily make women prettier, but rather mask her and strip her of her natural beauty.

Such spending as this is not proper while millions of people are dying of starvation. Women spend astronomical amounts to look good for men, and the irony is that she does not look good. It is a false perception that the whole world has bought into. In reality, we are misappropriating funds to cosmetic products. For example, in 2004, American spent more than 17 trillion dollars just for cosmetic products and perfumes. Do we really need the cologne or the perfume so we can smell good? How about our natural smell? We need to feel the pheromones of each other, so we can be attracted sexually.

The latest scientific research shows that males and females are encountering low libido, and that is attributed to the wide spread use of cologne or perfumes.

According to evolution, we need to pick up on the scent of others and differentiate between the people we like and those we don't. The use of cosmetics has caused quite a lot of sexual suffering. It masks everything, and we need to come back to our original nature and stop using all these chemical products.

The other danger of using cosmetics is its pollution to the environment. Most cosmetics are all chemical and most of it is poisonous. Eventually, these chemicals enter the soil and groundwater, and pollute vegetation, water, land and the air. Thus, we are committing a crime against ourselves, as well as future generations. We are polluting our environment with chemicals, just to dye our hair or put cosmetics and scents on our body, which seals the pores in our skin, and make them unable to breathe. Consequently that age us quickly and thereby develop wrinkles on our face and body.

Our mindless spending for beauty products has serious consequences on us as a society, such as:

1. Low libido, which causes marital problems, depression and anxiety primarily with the male. A man is a vulnerable creature when it comes to his sexuality. Women are not, because they are stronger sexually. A man worries about his sexual performance, and women are not that concerned about theirs, because they can fake orgasm without their partner ever knowing.
2. Pollution to the whole environment. We spend huge amounts of money on beauty products when people are suffering from disease, starvation, lack of clean water, or

the basic necessities of life. Do we really, as rational beings, know our priorities? Are we concerned about our fellow humans? Are we concerned about future generations? If we are not able to face ourselves, and correct the situation we have created for hundreds of years, then we basically are not rational beings, and we are fabulously stupid and idiots, because we are seeking our own destruction.

We do not need to make women in a false image, just to please the opposite sex, and we do not need to spend all that money doing so. In reality, there is nothing more beautiful than natural beauty. For example, we like the forest, because it looks very natural, and we do not like plastic trees, because they are not natural. Thus, a woman who looks natural is far better than a woman who has slathered her body and face with unattractive chemical color.

Fresh face or just a waste? The cosmetic and skincare industries are billion dollar booming segments of the economy, even though most of their products contain carcinogens and harsh chemicals. It has heavily impacted our environment as these are washed off our faces and washed down our drain. *Time* magazine recently stated there is no one aspect of the skincare and cosmetic industries that has not been cause for environmental concern.

If you think that an average woman uses between 10 and 15 cosmetic products on a given day, and the average man uses up to 6, the impact of synthetic chemicals and other forms of waste can be nothing but immense. Figures released by the U.S. EPA and Census Bureau show that more than 3 million tons of personal care chemicals are dumped into waterways each year. With so much of our waste disposed of in this way, it is very difficult to determine just how much of an environmental impact cosmetics and skincare products alone create. But with the increased amounts of waste products by these industries, one can only assume that the irreversible damage to our ecosystem is partly due to the chemicals found in everyday items.

For example, DDT, Sodium lauryl sulphate, Hydroquinone, contained in cosmetics, and the plastic packaging used are disposed of in our water and affect the breeding patterns of fish. In the U.S. alone, one third of landfill waste comes from beauty and skincare products. What's more, on a yearly basis we 38,000,000 animals are used to test beauty products.

In the United States alone, the frightening reality is that around 89% of the ingredients found in everyday items have not been assessed for safety against any publicly accountable institutions; even the FDA has no authority to check the safety record. Americans spend billions on unproven creams, gels, and ointments. Some products claim to have been tested, but by pseudo-scientific methods, which often find the product is "safe".

A team of researchers from the University of Wisconsin–Superior discovered that many plastic samples taken from the lake were micro-sized spherical plastic balls of the kind used in products such as facial and body scrubs (Marine Pollution Bulletin). It is a horrifying finding that makes us very vulnerable to disease and contamination. This is one of the reasons we spend huge amounts of money on our healthcare system, but yet illness is on the increase, because of the toxicity in our environment.

It is a sad reality that to make a woman's face "fresh", we have to commit a heinous crime toward our environment and our health. How stupid that we want to make our faces fresh but in the process, we make our immune system susceptible to all kinds of diseases. This is the human paradox: we fix one part of the body, but we damage others. In the final analysis, we have to speak directly to women, and ask them to stop using any kind of cosmetic products to save our health and our environment. And, we can spend that money in improving the health of people and feeding starving people around the world. Because, God created you complete and nothing is missing in you, thus you do not need to use makeup, because, makeup is making up for something missing. There is nothing missing in you, you are beautiful in your body as well as in your soul!

A final take home message and urgent call. Using cologne and perfume affects on our sexuality; the scientific explanation is that these products have masked our pheromones, which is the sexual scent that we all have. This natural body scent makes us appealing to the opposite sex. This is how the Antes behaved this way. They followed each other as a result of the scent they produced. So long as we slather our body with unnatural products sexual desire will be in decline.

So, in the final analysis, using cosmetic products is similar to armaments; both of them are a waste, and drain our national resources. Both of them are toxic to Mother Earth, and both are deceptions to the real morality of humankind, claiming something that is not real.

Chapter Eighteen

Jealousy

Jealousy is one of the most powerful human emotions. It is a complex emotion that encompasses many different kinds of feelings, which range from fear of abandonment, to rage, to humiliation. Jealousy can strike both men and women, when they perceive a third party threat to a valued relationship. It can be a problem among siblings competing for parental attention, or envy for wealthier, more successful friends. Conventional wisdom holds that jealousy is a necessary emotion because it preserves social bonds, but jealousy usually does more harm than good to a relationship, and can create conflicts and violence within that relationship.

Jealousy is deeply ingrained in human nature, and occurs in everyone's life, with varying intensity and significance. What is profoundly puzzling is, jealousy provokes humans to irrational, sometimes violent acts against others or against themselves. It's a passion that fascinates all of us. Jealousy is a reaction to a perceived threat -- real or imagined -- to a valued relationship or to its quality. A nationwide survey of marriage counselors indicated that jealousy is a problem in one-third of all couples coming for marital therapy. Occasionally, people may seek revenge from a perceived threat.

Is jealousy a form of madness? Jealousy lies somewhere in the gray area between sanity and madness. Some jealous reactions are so natural that a person who does not show them seems, in some way, not normal. Others seem so excessive that one does not need to be an expert to know they are pathological. A classic example is the man who is suspicious of his loving and faithful wife, so he constantly spies on her, listens to her phone conversations, records the mileage in her car for unexplained trips, and despite her repeated proof of fidelity, continues to suspect her, and he suffers tremendous jealousy.

Jealousy has sickening combinations of possession, suspicion, rage, and humiliation. It can overtake our mind and threaten our very core as you contemplate your rival. "The green-eyed monster", is what Shakespeare called it. Jealousy can camp in your head at any time during a relationship, when you are madly in love, or you have a snuggle attachment, or even when you dislike your partner. Jealousy bedevils other creatures.

Why do we feel jealous and how does it work? People who feel inadequate, insecure, or overly dependent tend to be more jealous than others. And, we tend to experience the feeling of jealousy when someone flirts with your partner, when someone achieves something that you have always wanted to achieve but did not manage yet, when someone you hate succeeds, when someone manages to get something, yet thinking he does not deserve it. Of all human emotions, jealousy is the most common and unsettling. It tends to bring out the worst in us, even if we know better. It is an age-old problem, and not limited just to humans. Wild animals, like chimpanzees, elephants and camels, can exhibit jealousy tendencies. Human history is filled with stories about jealousy, like the story of Greek goddess Hera, wife to the philandering Zeus. So if jealousy impacts humans negatively, why do we continue to behave this way? Cultural psychologists are of the opinion that we are inherently jealous people, and yet it may preserve the bonds of a relationship.

Jealousy is hard wired into our DNA. The green-eyed monster of jealousy may be hardwired into our DNA, but there is much we can do to keep it under control. The first study to investigate the genetic influence on jealousy was recently published. Researchers distributed questionnaires to more than 3,000 pairs of Swedish twins. Fraternal twins share about 50% of their genes; identical twins share exactly the same genetic make up. By comparing the answers given by each set of twins, researchers were able to show that, across the population, around one-third of the different levels of jealousy are likely to be genetic in origin.

Elizabeth Bowen once wrote, "jealousy is no more than feeling alone against smiling enemies. Others are overtly joyful or secretly mocking, while we are left alone to look a fool. Jealousy itself can take on a sort of wicked presence in our lives. Action taken in its behalf have been known to crush a budding romance, slowly erode a longstanding union or even lead to serious abuse."

Jealousy is not something we have much control over. It is a natural, instinctive emotion that everyone experiences at one point or another. The problem with jealousy is that it masks other feelings and attitudes that are even more hurtful to us and those closest to us. Its intensity is often shielding deep-seated feelings of passiveness, insecurity, and shame. What lies at the heart of jealousy very often is not the threat itself, but a drive we have within us to torment ourselves and berate ourselves with self-critical thoughts.

The irrationality of jealousy. Think about the thoughts we have when we feel jealous, lurking behind the paranoia toward our partner, or the criticism towards a third party threat, or even critical thoughts about ourselves. Our critical inner voice turns on us, and on those closest to us, when we notice ourselves fostering unwarranted suspicion or accusing our partner of being distracted, rejected, insensitive, or cruel.

For example, when we search our partner's cell phone for suspicious texts or restrict our partner from having friends, we are acting on our old self-doubt and mistrust that has nothing to do with current circumstances. If we do then find a text message from an ex in our partner's phone, or hear that our partner is out with an attractive co-worker at a company event, we may overreact in a way that neither we nor our partner are likely to respect.

Understanding the roots of jealousy. Identifying the triggers and reasons for our jealousy are an important part of maintaining a healthy relationship. To do this, we must be aware of the critical inner voice driving our uncertainty and self-doubt. If we can identify these thoughts, we can challenge them as "smiling enemies". They are the ones that want us to wind up alone. We have to challenge those thoughts, and that may initially make us anxious; we may even intensify verbal attacks in the short run. In the long run it will strengthen us as individuals and improve our trust and communication with our partner. The more we weaken this internal enemy, the more we strengthen a positive sense of self. This will enable us to accept the reality that we are loved, and reject the misperception that we are going to be betrayed. Jealousy alerts us to a looming problem in our relationship. Jealousy is pointlessly corrosive, making both partners miserable for no good reason. We need to get the better of jealousy.

Often, the feeling of jealousy can go seriously awry. We become consumed by it, undermining self-esteem, and even driving our partner into another's arms, which is the very outcome we had feared. Indeed, jealousy is a leading cause of spousal homicide worldwide.

The dynamic of jealousy. The unique dynamic of a relationship can affect jealousy. For example, if there is a mismatch in the relationship, it can be a recipe for jealousy. Insecure attachment can play a very tricky role in a relationship; people with insecure attachment are more jealous than people who have a secure attachment. For example, a husband who needs a lot of attention and reassurance might be more prone to jealousy, if his wife tends to like her personal space. Or a highly social husband may make his introverted wife more jealous.

The first cases of human jealousy. When God created Adam, He asked all the angels and Lucifer to treat the new creature

Adam with respect. Unfortunately, Lucifer refused, because he felt jealous that God was giving preferential treatment to Adam and did not give the rest of heaven's inhabitants with no such privileges. At this point, jealousy rose within Lucifer and he refused the order of God to show respect to Adam. Consequently, God expelled Adam and Eve from heaven because of their defiance to God's order, and also expelled Lucifer because of his jealousy of Adam, and his refusal to show respect. Undoubtedly, that was the beginning of human suffering, and jealousy was the central motivator.

The second case of jealousy that helped shaped human psychology, was the jealousy of Cain toward his brother Abel, both sons of Adam. Cain's jealousy eventually led to the murder of his brother. Cain felt very jealous of Abel for several reasons, and he committed murder. Sadly, Adam did nothing to stop the sibling rivalry between his sons. Ironically, Adam's family was a very dysfunctional one. Thus, the start of the universe was filled with jealousy, the cause of most of our misery, as we inherited it. Needless to say, jealousy can be considered one of the major causes of the enormous problems in our relationships today. Jealousy originated from the wicked side of our self, or arose from the dark side of our soul.

What are the causes behind jealousy? In the spectrum of human emotions, jealousy is almost certainly one of the most complex, frustrating and uncomfortable. This cocktail of anger, sadness, suspicion, and envy can destroy relationships, cause depression and anxiety, and even lead to violence in the form of homicide. There are specific causes for jealousy:

1. Jealousy's root cause is the lack of self-confidence, when we are not sure about ourselves;
2. Poor self-image is also a root cause of jealousy;
3. The fear of being alone, fear of ending a relationship, fear of being rejected, fear of loving someone else.

Jealousy arises in loving relationships because of comparison, competition and fear of being replaced. But if we become more autonomous and self-creating, these three features of a relationship become less significant, and hence the passion of jealousy becomes less likely. The bitter feeling of jealousy can hurt us and lead to hostility; it is a powerful obsession in life. The link between jealousy, aggression and low self-esteem, as Jeffery Parker indicated in his research, is that often, with intimacy comes vulnerability. Since we are vulnerable when we get into a relationship, jealousy visits us, and makes our lives full of misery and disappointment .

Jealousy and envy. Although these two words are used synonymously, they refer to different emotions. Jealousy refers to the fear of losing someone or something you value., It is a hard-wired emotion, developed through evolution, and evolution psychology has written extensively about the role of jealousy in mating strategies. Envy is resentment over something you do not have but want. It is a misconception that jealousy and envy are interchangeable. Envy wants something that someone else has, while jealousy more aptly describes an anticipatory emotion; it seeks to prevent loss. Dr. Ralph Hupka says that jealousy causes us to take precautionary measures. Should those fail and our partner has an affais, the new situation arouses anger, depression, and disappointment.

The core of jealousy. People do not experience jealousy unless they feel threatened by another person or entity, and fear being replaced. For example, sibling jealousy is usually caused by a child's fear that his parents will replace him with a new sibling, or love another sibling more. In romance, jealousy is typically triggered by third party. The third party does not have to actually pose a threat; the mere perception of a threat are enough to get the wheel of jealousy turning.

Jealousy can give couples an opportunity to examine two key questions:

1. What is the essence of your love? What was it that attracted you to each other initially, and what is the most important thing that holds the relationship together?

2. What is the shadow that your love casts when threatened? What is the threat that causes a jealous response in the other person?

Delusional jealousy (the Othello Syndrome.) It is very important to differentiate normal jealousy from delusional jealousy. Normal jealousy has its basis in a real threat to a relationship. Delusional jealousy persists despite the absence of any real or even probable threat. Sometimes delusional jealousy is called morbid jealousy, also known as the Othello Syndrome. It is a psychopathological condition in which a person holds a strong delusional belief that their spouse or sexual partner is being unfaithful, without having any significant proof to back up their claim. It is a delusion and obsession, and is also a type of mental illness that involves psychosis. The operational definition of delusional jealousy is a false belief, based on incorrect inference about external reality, that is firmly sustained despite what almost everyone else believes.

The name Othello Syndrome comes from the Shakespeare play "Othello". In that story, Othello murders his beautiful wife Desdemona, because he believes her unfaithful. It is a syndrome mostly associated with a neurological disorder, because usually there is no evidence to support this suspicion.

Psychosis is a break with reality, and involves the inability to distinguish what is real from what isn't. A delusion is the belief that something is real, despite evidence to the contrary. An individual with delusional jealousy may experience bizarre delusions, in which he believes that someone is being poisoned, followed, conspired against, or admired from a distance. There are six types of delusion disorders, and jealousy is one of them. An individual who suffers from delusional jealousy believes that his partner or spouse is cheating, in the absence of evidence to support that belief.

Individual psychological factors. Like almost every other emotion and relationship problem, jealousy is heavily affected by individual factors. Past experiences can increase a person's likelihood of being jealous. If our parents modeled jealousy, we may become more jealous. If we experienced betrayal by a lover, we might be more prone to suspicion, anxiety, and worry all of which increase the tendency to be jealous. Part of it depends on the quality of the relationship; some people may be more jealous than others, but virtually everyone is jealous in an unstable or unloving relationship.

Jealousy is centered on the fear of losing someone. If you are unsure of your spouse's love, or a child is not clear whether his parents still love him, despite having new siblings, then jealousy is more likely to become explosive. If a relationship is troubled, jealousy my surface and add yet another burden to the relationship. If we look to gender, age, ethnicity, or other factors, women are more inclined to be jealous more often, simply because they tend to be more honest and in touch with their emotions than their counterparts.

Empirical evidence suggests that male sexual jealousy is the leading cause of spousal battering. Studies of shelters documented that in the majority of cases, women cite extreme jealousy on the part of their husband or boyfriends as the key cause for spousal abuse. As repugnant as this may be, some men beat their wives to deter them from consorting with other men. Sexual jealousy appears to be another key context, triggering sexual aggression and homicide. It is primarily men who do the killing, and other men who are the victims.

Penis envy. Freud came up with the concept in which a female is envious of male characteristics or capabilities, especially the possession of a penis. He described the displeasure experienced by young girls when they realize they lack a penis. He also described the attempts those girls take over the course of their lives to compensate for the missing penis through such acts as childbearing and other achievements. During the pre-Oedipal stages, both the boy and the girl develop negative feelings of jealousy, hostility and rivalry toward the parent of the same sex, but different mechanisms for the parent of the opposite sex. A boy's attachment to his mother becomes stronger, and he starts developing negative feelings of rivalry and hostility toward his father, so the boy can become his mother's unique love object. On the other hand, a girl starts a love relationship with her father. The mother is seen by the girl as a competitor for the father's love and so the girl develops feelings of hostility and jealousy toward her mother.

How to manage jealousy. Zawan Villines, in his research, indicated that jealousy is not always a negative emotion. It can alert you to a deficit in your relationship and help you become mindful of potential outside threats. Jealousy can occur for no apparent reason. It can be highly destructive, but there are few steps you can follow to reduce the intensity of jealousy:

1. Talk directly and openly about feelings;
2. Discuss strategies to minimize jealousy;
3. Practice honesty in interpersonal relationships;
4. Examine whether the jealousy is caused by external or internal factors;
5. Work to improve a lack of emotion within;
6. Take time to make people feel valuable and trustworthy;
7. Desensitization, in which you write down all your spouses behaviors that instigate your jealousy, and examine it closely. In cases like this, you will need some professional help to accomplish this.

In extreme cases, the individual must be willing to undergo a psychological evaluation and treatment for jealousy, but jealousy can be very difficult to treat and it may take a long time. Sometimes, the patient can become worse, in frequency and intensity. Cognitive therapy may help change the patient's thinking process. A psychologist can help the patient find alternative theories that offer different explanations besides infidelity. Sadly the accusation of infidelity is more common among men in a traditional culture.

How the green-eyed monster can be tamed:

1. Consider the evidence for your jealousy, then find evidence to contradict your fears. Have a chat with a trusted friend to get an independent perspective on how likely it is that your partner is deceiving you.
2. Talk to your partner about the people in their life.
3. Weigh the pros and cons of the relationship.
4. Get to the bottom of your fears. Do you dread being alone? Do you fear humiliation? What is fueling your jealousy?
5. Think constructively about how to handle the situation.
6. Set some ground rules. We find ourselves trapped in a vicious cycle; jealous behavior feeds jealous thoughts, which in turn trigger more jealous behavior .
7. Concentrate on the good stuff. Jealousy skews our perspective; focus on the good part of the relationship, because in the end it is all in the mind of the jealous person.
8. If all else has failed, then the intervention of a professional psychologist is clearly indicated, and necessary to the survival of the relationship.

Chapter Nineteen

Human Aggression & Violence

Aggression is intentional behavior aimed at doing harm or causing pain to another person or group. Hostile aggression is aggression stemming from a feeling of anger and aimed at inflicting pain. Bear in mind, anger is not the same as aggression. Aggression is a perplexing phenomenon. Why are people motivated to hurt each other? How does violence help organisms survive and produce? We need to look deep, psychologically and evolutionally, to the roots of aggression, as well as its consequences on society.

Social psychology defines aggression as behavior whose immediate intent is to hurt someone; or it can be a conflict between two parties. Aggression and violence by one human toward another is not a new phenomenon; it's been prevalent since the dawn of time. But, technology has made mass violence far easier to accomplish. It is doubtful that people are more violent today than a thousand years ago. But, the prevalence of aggression and violent behavior today is sufficient to make it a social problem worthy of investigation.

Aggression can be used to defend against attacks. Aggression may be an effective solution to one's resources being forcibly taken. It can be used to cultivate a reputation that deters others from taking advantage of the aggressive party. It can be used to prevent loss of status and honor that would otherwise follow being victimized.

The start of human aggression. The start of human aggression comes from Adam, who initiated his aggression toward the order of our Almighty God, when he defied the order of God and committed the grave sin, resulting in our expulsion from the paradise of Eden. Adam's aggression was perpetuated by his son Cain who murdered his brother Abel. Undoubtedly, that was the start of human aggression and humanity has followed that disturbing course ever since. We wage wars against each other, as individuals or as groups or even as nations. For example, in recent history the human community has waged World War I and World War Two, which took millions and millions of lives of innocent people. People have also committed savage atrocities, as well as destroyed hundreds of cities. Sadly, aggression is a tendency that has woven itself into the fabric of the human psyche.

Evolution psychology and aggression. All our behaviors originated through the process of evolution, by natural or sexual selection. Selection is the only causal process powerful enough to produce complex organic mechanisms. From evolution's perspective, aggression is the beast within; survival of the fittest has bred aggression in humans. Thus, it is human nature to be aggressive. There are within us psychological mechanisms and motives that orient our behavior. Evolution tells us that in nature, man is physically and verbally more aggressive than woman, because humans strive for mastery of material resources, as well as for respect and connection to others.

Aggression is regarded as highly context-specific, triggered only in a context in which specific adaptive problems are confronted, and the adaptive benefits are likely to be reaped. For example, there's aggression toward stepchildren, including aggression which falls short of actual homicide. Since the presence of stepchildren threatens to absorb valuable resources that might otherwise get channeled to genetically related child, adult aggression against stepchildren has an evolutionary function, which is to reduce the resources spent on unrelated children.

In evolution, within the context of small group, a loss of status is catastrophic in the currency of survival and reproduction, because we carry with us ancient psychological mechanisms for aggression, designed for a time and place long forgotten. Present aggressive behavior may be maladaptive today, just as our taste for fatty foods may be maladaptive in a modern environment characterized by fast food restaurants on every corner. The mechanisms operate nonetheless, triggered by events that would have triggered them in our ancestral past.

Psychoanalysis and aggression. Freud indicated the deepest essence of human nature is similar in all men. This essence is aimed at the satisfaction of certain needs, such as self-preservation, aggression, the need for love, and the impulse to attain pleasure and avoid pain. Men are wolves to each other; men are not gentle creatures who want to be loved. Man has a powerful share of aggressiveness. As a result, a neighbor is for him not only a potential helper or sexual object, but also someone who tempts him to satisfy his aggression; to exploit his capacity for work without compensation, to use him sexually without his consent, to seize his possessions, to humiliate him, to cause him pain, to torture him, as well as to kill him (Freud). No doubt, such views of human nature by Freud are not romantic ones, but are a very gloomy one. But, that is the reality of human psychology.

Freud went further and said, (who in the face of all his experiences of life and history will have the courage to dispute this assertion), "once you provoke man then he spontaneously reveals his savage beast nature." The best testimonials for that, are the atrocities committed during the racial migration of the Huns, or the Mongols under Genghis Khan and Tamerlane, or the capture of Jerusalem by savage Crusaders, even the horrors of World Wars One and Two, or the terrorists of today in the Arab world and Afghanistan.

Freud asserted that human behavior is motivated by sexuality, an instinctive drive known as libido. It is an energy derived from the Eros, or life instinct. Thus, the repression of such libidinal urges is displayed as aggression. He also developed the concept of

Thanatos, or the death force, which is contrary to the libido energy emitted from the Eros. Thanatos energy encourages destruction and death.

Analytical psychotherapy has clinically demonstrated that people have unconscious homicide, suicidal, and destructive aggressive fantasies and dreams. But the person with a well-functioning set of ego boundaries does not act out these fantasies. In the neurotic personality, aggression permeates all aspects of the personality. Furthermore, the death instinct is considered to be active aggression against the self, according to Freud.

Melanie Klein in 1931 indicated that the origin of aggression is the unresolved feelings of Oedipal hostility, which is desire and aggression at the same time towards the opposite sex. A daughter has a desire to be with her father, and has aggression toward her mother; the son has a desire to be with his mother, and has aggression toward the father. If we do not resolve this conflict, we carry it to adulthood and it crystallizes into aggression and hostility.

Carl Jung in 1933 hypothesized that violence and destructive aggression was an unleashing of a primordial archetypical behavior, inherent in the collective unconscious minds of people throughout ages. An extrovert will act out his aggression against others or against the environment, whereas the violently aggressive introverted person will be self–destructive and perhaps suicidal. A person, in whom thinking is the superior function, exerts intellectual control over aggression. In contrast, the person in whom feeling is the superior function is more likely to express aggression overtly. Finally, some archaic experiences occur in a number of culture experiences, such as the passion to spill blood -- bloodlust -- may fit Jung's concept of the racial unconscious and archetype.

The biology of aggression. The energy of aggression is an instinctual drive that builds until it explodes. It may be released by external stimuli, but its internal building quality guarantees that it will be pushed out, one way or another. All human behavior is a product of these internal mechanisms, in conjunction with input that triggers the activation of those mechanisms. Even the simplest behavior, such as a blink of the eyes in response to a puff of air, requires both a mechanism and input.

The other explanation of aggression is Darwinian natural selection. Since the healthier and stronger animals eliminate weaker ones, over the course of evolution the result is an ultimately stronger, healthier population. Empirical evidence shows that cerebral electrical stimulation of certain locations in the brain can induce or inhibit aggression. Other biological theories propose there are genetic components to aggression. Other biological evidence of aggression is the neurotransmitters, such as serotonin, dopamine and noradrenalin, which produce high level of aggression in animals. Hence, the Amygdale and the Hypothalamus are the areas in the brain which trigger aggression.

Hostile world schemes, maladaptive families, poor parenting, and low serotonin may produce heightened levels of aggression, as well as high testosterone, executive functioning deficit, low IQ or low emotional intelligence, or attention deficit and hyperactivity disorder (ADHD). All these contribute to the aggressive tendency within human species.

Aggression versus violence. Aggression as a behavior is directed toward another individual, and carried out with the intent to cause harm. Violence is physical aggression at the extremely high end of the aggression continuum, such as murder and aggravated assault. All violence is aggression, but some aggression is not violence. And the causes for both are environmental and biological modifiers.

Culture and aggression. David Buss, the professor of psychology who investigated evolution, has indicated that aggression has a long evolutionary history in the human psyche. Hence, in Western society, aggression can be invoked by modern living, like the violence in movies, television, or the toys with which kids play. All these media tools can develop observational learning. The rate of suicide is commonly high among traditional societies, such as the Ache Indians of Paraguay and the Tiwi of Northern Australia. Victims of aggression can also lose in the currency of status and reputation. The loss of face or honor entailed by being abused with impunity, can lead to further abuse by others.

Negative status and power hierarchies in modern societies may be a great contributor to aggression. Furthermore, we have ritualized aggression in the form of boxing, or in wrestling. For example, in these sports, the victor experiences status elevation and the loser a status loss. Men who expose themselves to danger in warfare to kill enemies are regarded as brave and courageous, and consequently experience an elevation in their status within a group. The hypothesis that aggression sometimes serves the adoptive function of status elevation does not imply that this strategy work in all groups. Deterring rivals from future aggression with aggression may deter aggression and other forms of cost–inflicting from others.

Gender difference in human aggression. Men and woman both derogate their same-sex rivals, impugning their status and reputation to make them less desirable to members of the other sex. But, why is man more aggressive than woman? In research conducted in Chicago about homicides committed from 1965 to 1980, 86% were committed by males (Daly & Wilson, 1980). In all culture studies, men are overwhelmingly more often the killer, and their victims are mostly other men. Evolution explains that in the model of inter-sexual competitiveness. It starts with parental investment and sexual selection. In a species in which females invest more heavily in offspring than males, females become the valuable limiting resource on reproduction for males. Males become constrained in their reproduction not so much by their ability to survive, but by their ability to gain sexual access to the high-investment females. The female bears the burdens of internal fertilization, placentation, and gestation.

Man has inherited from his successful ancestors psychological mechanisms, sensitive to contexts in which aggression probability leads to the successful solution of a particular adoptive problem. Males are more often the perpetrators of violence because they are the products of a long history of mild but sustained effective polygyny characteristics by risking strategies of inter-sexual competition for access to high-investment sex. The fact that men die on average 7 years earlier than women, is but one of the many markers of this aggressive inter-sexual strategy. Thus, men are the victims of aggression far more than women, because men are in competition primarily with other men.

Women though, also engage in aggression, and their victims are also typically members of their own sex. In studies of verbal aggression through derogation of competitors, for example, woman slander their rivals by impugning their physical appearance and hence reproductive values (Buss, Dedden, 1999). Man's aggression against men worldwide reveals the majority of killers are men, and mostly the killers share similar characteristics, such as being unemployed, and unmarried. A Detroit homicide study in 1982 explained that lacking resources, and being unable to attract long-term mates, appeared to be the social contexts for male-male homicides, especially when men want to compete for status and mating.

Overall, women's physical aggression is less than men's. However, the low level of risking physical aggression does not translate into a low level of verbal aggression. If we define aggression as inflicting costs on someone else, women's aggression can be quite potent. Women engaged in as much verbal aggression against their rivals as did men. Woman exceeded men in derogating their rivals on the bases of physical appearance and sexual promiscuity; they call each fat, ugly and physically unattractive. Women seem to be extraordinary observant about the physical imperfections in other women's appearances, and take pains in the context of inter-sexual competition.

The most repugnant type of aggression is against women who have engaged in premarital sex. The reason for such an "honor killing" is that man would like to have a monopoly over a woman's sexuality. In the Arab culture they tie sexuality to the sense of honor, and if a woman loses her virginity, she will bring shame to the whole family. But if a man is promiscuous, there is no such cultural shame that attaches to him or his family.

Arabs feel that women carry the honor of the family; in particular, her sexuality is the most precious thing, and valued highly. Since women carry that huge burden, the consequences of losing virginity can lead to killing the woman. This sort of aggression is still practiced in some societies in the Arab world. It is the most ridiculous and stupid practice committed against women. Arab society needs to free themselves from such nonsensical cultural practices. They need to reexamine the concept of honor and sexuality, and try to distance them from each other. Sex is a basic need, like food and drink; what has it to do with honor? Or they may have to treat men's and, women's sexuality the same, without putting a premium on a woman's sexuality, but allowing men to have casual sex without consequences. By doing that they remove the stigma from women's sexuality.

Other understandings of the causes of aggression. In frustration theory, John Dollard came up with this concept, linking frustration to aggression. He discovered prisoners who are frustrated may become aggressive. But it can be a weak instigator, and can be defined as the blockage of goal attainment. Bad moods may also produce a negative effect, and serve as an instigator of aggression. Contrary to popular belief, low self-esteem is not a good predictor of aggression. Individuals with inflated or unstable high self-esteem are the most prone to anger, and are the most aggressive people, especially when their high self-esteem is threatened.

The social learning theory has different perspectives about aggression, positing that aggression is not caused by internal mechanisms, but by socially learned behavior and maintained by other conditions. For example, the influence of the media, television, movies, and video games all are work to reinforce aggression. The violence in the media is overwhelming to young people, and makes them nervous. Consequently, they may imitate what they see, like observational learning. Thus, according to this concept aggression is a learned behavior and not genetically inherited.

Alfred Adler in 1908 speculated about aggression, and he first proposed the idea that aggression was an innate, primary instinctual drive. He said all behavior stemmed from aggression (as a masculine protest against feelings of inferiority), with sexuality being reduced to man's aggressive attempt to master women. Adler also postulated that the beginning of aggression started with sibling rivalry as one of the basic behavioral motivations. Cain's murder Abel and the story of Jacob and his son Esau are the best examples.

Aggression can be sadistic, with the desire to have absolute control over others, or masochistic, in wanting to be completely under others' control. Or, it can be a passion to destroy and tear apart living things. Sadism is imbedded in the fabric of our conscious and unconscious mind, and it tends to show up in many forms of abuse and hostility. We see a mass sadism when a nation attacks another nation and inflicts enormous suffering and pain, often without any shred of mercy. That is the ugly face of the human species.

Eric Fromm, who sees aggression as rooted in a death instinct, also saw that man's character is malignant and destructive. He distinguished between benign aggression and malignant aggression. Benign aggression is defensive against any attacks, and is built-in in animals and humans. Lorenz and Freud saw aggression as largely negative, hostile and destructive. Fromm sees aggression as instinctual, and that it can be positive, contributing to man's growth, self-assertion, and independence, and thus, to the survival of the species.

Gustavo Le Bon came up with the concept of the mob psychology. Once the individual becomes part of a group, he regresses to a primitive mental state, and behaves like a barbarian, prone to violence. He abandons his critical sense, becomes emotional, and loses all his moral standards, and inhibitions. His unique individual features disappear and a common ancestral heritage in man's unconscious becomes dominant. This stems from social anxiety and fear of others; it is mass hypnosis, and individuals become vulnerable to suggestion. In the group dynamic of aggression, individual members are subjected to a hypnotic spell, and the leader becomes each individual's ego ideal, to whom he hands over his basic critical faculties, just as the hypnotized individual abandons his self–determination to the control of the hypnotist. Freud was convinced that humans have a profound emotional need for strong leadership, or someone to control them.

In conclusion, aggression and violence dominate our human psyche to maximum capacity with murders, wars, exploitation, colonization, enslaving people, and abusing the poor and disadvantaged. Thus, we must regard aggression as a summated response to many factors. On an individual level, aggression is not at such a high level, but once we are united or act collectively, we truly unleash incredible aggression and violence, which causes terrible crimes and takes the lives of many innocent people. Thus, aggression is part and parcel of our psychological makeup, and if we do not exercise some control over it, aggression will sweep us away to the degree that we will not be able to exercise control over our own humanity.

There is a conflict between self-destructive aggression and self-preservation; there is a fine line and we may cross it often. Self –destructive aggression is very common when we are engaged in many conflicts and wars, which all lead to self-destruction. But, there is also aggression which preserves us, and in which we have to partake so we can survive, if we can defend against some attacks, or stop others from abusing us. The world today operates like a wolf and sheep. If you are a sheep, then there will be no excuse for the wolf in you to eat you alive. Thus, you need to protect yourself by being aggressive, or master the survival mechanism.

Conclusions

This book has investigated numerous phenomena of human destructive behavior, and we have seen how much such behaviors have contributed to human suffering and agony. If we take, for example, military spending, we see the amount of national resources that has been wasted and are still wasted is astonishing. Individually, we think there is no one in their right mind who can go that far and waste such precious resources in military machines, while half of our planet's people are hungry and sick, or living in subhuman conditions. Nonetheless, collectively, we encourage and reinforce the fear that dominates the human psyche, giving justification for military spending.

We conduct intelligent investigations, and try to answer why we behave destructively. There are myriad answers to that. But the most prominent answer is when God created the universe and humankind, the first program that was instilled in us was the human wicked inclination, before anything else. So, since God the Almighty instilled in us such a wicked program, then we are doomed from the start. You may go further and say that it's unfair that we came to this world with a bad start. As the existential thinkers put it very intelligently, our existence is merely a cruel trick.

The best testimonial for the bad start is Adam. Within seven days after his creation, he had disobeyed God's order and committed the grave sin, eating from the forbidden fruit. He did not wait long enough, did not ponder over it, and just followed his immature impulses, paralyzed by his desire or curiosity to know why he was being prevented. Yes, we are not far enough up the ladder of evolution, and were not ready to be expelled from heaven and come to earth, to shoulder the huge responsibility of being the guardians of the planet.

Needless to say, we have polluted every corner of the earth; we polluted the air, the ground, the water, and moreover, we have polluted our precious bodies. Sadly enough, we have all kinds of diseases that are destroying our bodies, as a result of the imbalanced life that we live. We all know illness can result from living an imbalanced life, physically, psychologically, or mentally, as well as spiritually. Modern medicine has segmented the three dominations of our totality, resulting in more disease, so the pharmaceutical companies can profit from our sickness.

Furthermore, we have polluted our minds with irrational thinking, which dominates our reasoning ability. Fear is also the other common denominator in the human psyche. Fear has paralyzed us, and taken all the joy out of life. It is becoming the prime motivator for our behavior. Undoubtedly, most of our fears are irrational and imagined, and very far from reality. But sadly, we treat fears as a real thing. Thus, we are suffering from anxiety, depression, obsessive thought, and most of all lack of enjoyment in our daily lives.

We are also suffering from emotional constipation. Our lives are becoming burdensome, not a journey of joy, which is what it is intended to be. Why are there a great number of people prone to depression and anxiety these days? The answer is that modern times are very advanced technologically and our brain is not designed to comprehend such advancement, or to cope with it. Our brain is still primitive, and was designed to be in the savanna or the jungle. Moreover, the advancement of technology, instead of bringing us closer together, has distanced us from each other. Human contact is becoming minimal. Thus modern man feels alienated, a stranger in his own home. Home is no longer a safe place for him; home is becoming a source of misery and unhappiness, because of marital unfulfillment, and unrewarding children.

If we also investigate religious dogma closely, we discover we are created initially with a wicked nature. In an effort to correct that, Almighty God sent numerous prophets and messengers to teach us basic human decency. Ironically, the religions that was supposed to salvage us, and bring to our life some relief from our wicked nature, has been twisted by man's evil nature and become the most disturbing element in our life. Nonetheless, the message from God was one of compassion and love.

People do not take the words of God seriously; it just reached their throats and stopped. They have developed their own perceptions of the words of God, resulting in the loss of the true meaning of God's messages. Thus, people today are fighting, not over the true meaning of the words, but over their own interpretations of the words of God. Therefore, we have witnessed incomprehensible atrocities throughout the history of mankind in the name of religion. Religion's twisted messages have caused us enormous pain and suffering. Unfortunately, there is no exit from it; it has to take its own cycle of violence.

Another part of human destructive behavior is when women us makeup to mask her true nature or looks. That is deceptive to man. Evolution psychology has indicated to us that man wants to see the true nature of woman, so he can choose her to be the mother of his children. But if she paints her face with all these chemicals, that is considered a form of deception and false to man.

Today even pretty women use all these chemicals, just as a part of fashion. It is toxic to our environment as well as to the woman's face. Women in general have fallen into the trap of believing that makeup makes her more beautiful or attractive, and that is absolutely false. It can even make her less attractive. On the top of that, she wastes a tremendous amount of time applying such chemicals over her face, as well as wasting money in such endeavors.

This book also addressed the tyranny of cultures as a part of human destructive behavior, and how to free oneself from the tyranny of the expected. Often culture expects us to be submissive to its practices, rules, and even to the collective thoughts of the culture. Consequently, in the process, you lose the essence of your individuality, and your creativity. You become a soulless person, or a pawn, allowing culture to dictate to you. Sooner or later, alienation may creep into your psyche, and you become frustrated, disappointed, and angry. That is what we see today, because of cultural tyranny. We see this often in the collectivist culture, but not so much in the individualistic culture.

That leads us to another topic this book has spelled out, which is the sheep mentality. Throughout human history, people crave to have a strong leader to follow, which means that in general, people like to be led, to be in the passenger seat, not in the driver's seat. When we behave that way, which entices some deviant personality to take advantage of this human tendency, and abuse us or subjugate us to all manner of humiliation. That is what has happened under dictators or despots. Those deviant personalities know the vulnerability of human psychology, and have used it to maximum effect. This is why human history is filled with all form of abuse and enslavement.

There are two parties involved in such a dance. One party is the majority of people who do not like to take control of their own lives, and hand their power to someone else. The other party is a small group of people who have dark souls that allow them to abuse their follow humans. So the majority of people are sheep, and there are few shepherds who take advantage of the rest by using and abusing them.

Painfully, that is the human condition. Since the Creation, there have been a lot of sheep, and a few wolves who lead them. What are the reasons behind such human behavior? The answer is a sad one: it is very difficult for the majority of people to take the initiative and take total control of their lives, because people by nature are lazy, irrational and mediocre. Therefore, they allow politicians or dictators to run their lives for them. That is the picture of human tragedy, as well part of the human destructive tendency.

References

Aristotle, (2001). *The Basic Works of Aristotle*. Modern Library Publisher, Reprinted Edition.

American Psychiatric Association, (2005). *Diagnostic And Statistical Manual of Mental Disorders*. American Psychological Association Press.

Al-Ghazzali (1997). *On Disciplining the Soul and Breaking the Two Desires*. Islamic Texts Society, Publisher.

Beck, Charlotte (2007). *Everyday Zen: Love & Work*. Harper One, Publisher.

Bazerman, H. Max (2012). *Judgment in Managerial Decision Making*. Wiley, Publisher.

Begley, Sharon (2007). *Train Your Mind, Change Your Brain*. Ballantine Books.

Bjorklund, F. David & Pellegrini, D. Anthony (2001). *The Origins of Human Nature*. American Psychological Association Press.

Blech, Jorg (2006). *Inventing Disease and Pushing Pills; Pharmaceutical Companies and the Medicalization of Normal Life*. Routledge, Publisher.

Bodenheim, Thomas (2006). *Improving Primary Care: Strategies and Tools for Better Practice*. McGraw-Hill Medical.

Bunge, Mario, (1998). *Philosophy of Science: From Problem to Theory*. Transactional, Publisher.

Burnham, Terry & Phelan, Jay (2000). *Mean Genes*. Perseus, Publisher.

Camus, Albert (1991). *The Myth of Sisyphus, and Other Essays*. Vintage, Reissue edition.

Carlson, Richard (1999). *Don't Sweat the Small Stuff*. Simon & Schuster, Publisher.

Chopra, Deepak & Tanzi, Rudolph (2012). *Super Brain*. Harmony Books, Publisher.

Cohen, Abraham (1995). *The Talmud: The Major Teachings of the Rabbinic Sages*. Schocken, Publisher.

Chomsky, Noam & Naiman, Arthur (2011). *How the World Works*. Soft Skull Press.

Cohen, Hillel (2009). *Army of Shadow: Palestinian Collaboration with Zionism*. University of California Press.

Dickens, Charles (2013). *Great Expectations*. Great Space Independent, Publisher.

Doidge, Norman (2007). *The Brain That Changes Itself*. Penguin Books.

Didion, Joan (2008). *Slouching Towards Bethlehem*. Farrar, Straus, & Giroux.

Ellis, A. (1974). *Rational–Emotive Theory*. Oxford, Brunner & Mosel, Publisher.

Eagleman, David (2012). *The Secret Life of the Brain*. Vintage, Publisher.

Fenichel, Otto (1945). *The Psychoanalytic Theory of Neurosis*. W. W. Norton & Company.

Freud, S. (1916). *Psychopathology of Everyday Life*. Macmillan, Publisher.

Freud, S. (1930). *General Introduction to Psychoanalysis*. Horace Liveright, Publisher.

Freud, S. (1946). *On Narcissism: An Introduction*. Modern Library, Publisher.

Freud, S. (1959). *Collected Papers*. Basic Books, Publisher.

Fromm, E. (1980). *The Heart of Man*. Harper Collins, Publisher.

Fromm, E. (1994). *Escape From Freedom*. Farrar & Rinehart, Publisher.

Fromm, E. (2006) *The Art of Loving*. Harper & Brothers, Publisher.

Fisher, Helen (1994). *Anatomy of Love: The Nature and Chemistry of Romantic Love*. Random House, Publisher.

Gibran, K. (1923). *The Prophet*. Penguin Books.

Gandhi, K. Mohandas (1980). *All Men Are Brothers*. Continuum, Publisher.

Goethe, Wolfgang Johann Van (1962) *Faust*. Anchor, Publisher.

Gray, John (2012). *Men are From Mars, Women are from Venus.* Harper Paperbacks, Publisher.

Hager, John (2005). The Only Sustainable Edge: Why business strategy depends on productive friction and dynamic specialization. Harvard Business Review.

Hemermesh, S. Daniel (2013). *Beauty Pays: Why Attractive People are More Successful.* Princeton University Press.

Horney, Karen (1981). *Neurosis and Human Growth: The Struggle Towards Self- Realization.* W.W. Norton & Company, Publisher.

Hippocrates (2006). *Health Program: A Proven Guide to Healthful Living.* Author Choice, Publisher.

Iacoboni, Marco (2009). *Mirroring People.* Farrar, Straus, & Giroux, Publisher.

Illich, Ivan (2000). *Deschooling Society.* Marion Boyars, Publisher.

Kahneman, Daniel (2011). *Thinking Fast and Slow* Farrar, Straus & Giroux, Publisher.

Kafaji, Talib (2011). *Inward Journey.* Author House Publishers, Indiana.

Kafaji, Talib (2011). *The Psychology of The Arab.* Author House Publishers, Indiana.

Kafaji, Talib (2013). *The Triumph Over the Mediocre Self.* Author House Publishers, Indiana.

Kierkegaard, Soren (1987). *Either/Or Part 1.* Princeton University Press.

Kant, Immanuel (2008). *Critique of Pure Reason.* Penguin Classics.

Kateb, George (2014). *Human Dignity.* Belknap Press.

Kendrick, Douglas (1964). Blood Program in World War II. Office of the Surgeon General, Department of the Army.

Knuston, Brian (2014). *The Interdisciplinary Science of Consumption.* MIT Press.

Krishnamurti, J. (2009). *Freedom From the Known.* Harper San Francisco, New Edition.

Laing, R. D. (1965). *The Divided Self: An Existential Study in Sanity and Madness.* Penguin Books.

Lama, Dalai (1998). *Buddha, The Fourth Noble Truth.*

Lewin, Kurt & Cartwright, Darwin (1951). *Field Theory In Social Science.*

May, Rolla (1969). *Love & Will.* W.W. Norton & Company.

Marx, Karl (2000). *Selected Writings.* Oxford University Press.

Machiavelli, Niccolo (1998). *The Prince.* University of Chicago Press, 2nd Edition.

Maurizio, Viroli (1997). *For Love of Country; An Essay on Patriotism and Nationalism.*
Oxford University Press.

Mason, Paul (2010). Meltdow : *The End of the Age of Greed.* Verso: New updated Edition.

Morris, Henry (1982). *Men of Science, Men of God*. Master Books, Publisher.

Moncrieff, Joanna (2009). *The Myth of the Chemical Cure: A Critique of Psychiatric Drug Treatment*. Palgrave Macmillan, Publisher.

Mercola, Joseph (2013). *Generation XL: Raising Healthy, Intelligent Kids in a High-Tech, Junk-Food World*. Thomas Nelson, Publisher.

Navia, E. Luis (2007). *Socrates: A Life Examined*. Prometheus Books.

Nietzsche, Friedrich (2000). *Basic Writings of Nietzsche*. Modern Library, Publisher.

Nesbitt, J. Richard (1993). *The ASW Ship System*. Society of Automotive Engineering.

Orwell, George (1984). *Animal Farm*. Houghton Mifflin Harcourt, Publisher.

Ornesh, Dean (1999). *Love and Survival: 8 Pathways to Intimacy and Health*. William Morrow Paperbacks, Publisher.

Plato (2002). *Five Dialogues*. Hackett, Publisher.

Paterson, William (2004). *The Man Who Saw the Future*. Texere, Publisher.

Peter, J. Laurence (2011). *The Peter Principle: Why Things Always go Wrong*. Harper Business, Publisher.

Pinker, Steven (2009). *How the Mind Works*. W.W. Norton & Company.

Prochaska, O. James & Diclement, Carlo (2007). *Changing for Good: A Revolutionary Six Stage Program for Overcoming Bad Habits and*

Moving Your Life Positively Forward. William Morrow Paperbacks, Publisher.

Ropeik, David (2010). *How Risky Is It, Really: Why Our Fears Do Not Always Match the Facts.* McGraw-Hill, Publisher.

Rousseau, Jean-Jacques (1992). *Discourse on the Origins of Inequality.* Hackett, Publisher.

Rushton, Philippe (1994). *Race, Evolution, and Behavior: A Life History Perspective.* Transactional Publishers.

Roger, Carl (1980). *A Way of Being.* Mariner Books.

Rantala, Markus (2014) How Feminine Is Your Girlfriend's Face? *Science* (29 April 2014)

Sartre, Jean-Paul (1989). *No Exit and Three Other Plays.* Vintage Reissue.

Schopenhauer, Arthur (1995). *The World as Will and Idea.* Everyman Paperbacks.

Shaw, George Bernard (2001). *Man and Superman.* Penguin Classics.

Sheehy, Gail (2010). *The Silent Passage.* Gallery Books.

Smith, T. Shawn (2011). The User's Guide to the Human Mind. New Harbinger Publications.

Spiel, Hilde (2008). *The Dark and The Bright: Memoirs.* Ariadne, Publisher.

Stawell, Melina (2010). *A Clue to the Cretan Scripts.* Kessinger Publishers, LLC.

Smith, Adam (2009). *The Wealth of Nations*. Thrifty Books, Publisher.

Tolstoy, Leo (2008). *War and Peace*. Vintage Classics Press.

Tzu, Lao (1990). *Tao Te Ching*. Harper Perennial Compact Edition.

Taflinger, F. Richard. (2010). *Taking Advantage*. Kendall Hunt, Publisher.

Vidal, Gore (2003). *The City and the Pillar*. Vintage Publishers.

Vonnegut, Kurt (1999). *Mother Night*. Dial Press.

Webster's New World Dictionary (1957). The World Publishing Company.

Webley, Paul & Lea, Stephen (2001). *The Economic Psychology of Everyday Life*. Psychology Press.

Wilde, Oscar (2003). *Complete Works of Oscar Wilde*. Collins, Collins. Classics Edition.

Wilson, Timothy (2009). *Social Psychology*. Pearson Press.

Wordsworth, William (2008). *The Major Works: Including the Prelude*. Oxford University Press.

Zimbardo, Philip (2008). *The Lucifer Effect: Understanding How Good People Turn Evil*. Random House Publishers.